WRITING FOR BROADCAST NEWS

WRITING FOR BROADCAST NEWS

A Storytelling Approach to Crafting TV and Radio News Reports

Charles Raiteri

ROWMAN & LITTLEFIELD PUBLISHERS, INC.
Lanham • Boulder • New York • Toronto • Oxford

ROWMAN & LITTLEFIELD PUBLISHERS, INC.

Published in the United States of America
by Rowman & Littlefield Publishers, Inc.
A wholly owned subsidiary of
The Rowman & Littlefield Publishing Group, Inc.
4501 Forbes Boulevard, Suite 200, Lanham, MD 20706
www.rowmanlittlefield.com

P.O. Box 317, Oxford OX2 9RU, UK

British Library Cataloguing in Publication Information Available

Library of Congress Cataloging-in-Publication Data
Raiteri, Charles
  Writing for broadcast news : a storytelling approach to crafting TV and radio news reports / by Charles Raiteri.
      p. cm.
  Includes bibliographical references and index.
  ISBN 0-7425-4027-8 (pbk : alk. paper)
  1. Television broadcasting of news—Authorship. 2. Radio journalism—Authorship. I. Title.
PN4784.T4R36 2005
  808'.06607—dc22

                              2005009533

Printed in the United States of America

♾ ™The paper used in this publication meets the minimum requirements of American National
Standard for Information Sciences—Permanence of Paper for Printed Library Materials, ANSI/NISO
Z39.48-1992.

Brief Contents

Detailed Contents

Preface

While it is true that journalism is being processed at microchip speed in this computer-driven age and "convergence" (see chapter 16) has become the watchword of change, people continue to be people with all of their attendant human problems and concerns. Those human problems and concerns are the stuff of every newscast ever written, and those yet to be. That is why this text focuses on the human, storytelling approach to writing news stories. A story is always about people, be it a joke about a man walking into a bar or a news bulletin informing us that the president has ordered the draft reinstated. Through storytelling, the reporter draws the audience into the story, rather than simply giving the audience a dispassionate list of facts.

Writing for Broadcast News is an introductory text intended to provide a practical and clearly defined "storytelling" approach to the writing and reporting of broadcast news for radio, TV, or online. The essentials are presented with a how-to emphasis on writing stories of human dimension.

The text contains case studies of work done by actual student reporters as examples of what to do and what not to do in building a structured broadcast news report. Chapter 2 lists and defines broadcast news terms. Chapter 12 consists of exercises designed to test student understanding of the humanizing method. Exercises are based on information drawn from actual news stories.

Finally, this text is the synthesis of my twenty years on the street as a TV reporter and twelve years in the classroom as a broadcast journalism teacher. It's the product of what I learned from my peers and what I learned from my students. It can help you achieve your goal, if indeed your goal is to become a writer of competent, even creative, scripts for broadcast news, or whatever aural or visual medium you decide to make your life's work.

CHAPTER 1

Style

PEOPLE ARE LISTENING

People are listening. They're listening to the words you write. If not now, they will be when you get into the business. For that reason, you need to keep three things in mind when writing your stories: (1) broadcasters both read and speak the words they write, (2) people hear the words broadcasters speak, and (3) the words broadcasters speak must sound conversational.

Writers of broadcast news have developed a certain way of writing that facilitates those three goals. It's a way of writing designed to make sure our sentences fit our mouths and the listener's ears. It's called broadcast style.

Writers of broadcast news know people absorb news through a different sense when they listen to it than when they read it. Be it TV or radio, broadcast news is a spoken-word medium. In other words, broadcasters are talking to people, *telling* them the news. People get their news via the ear. Yes, with TV they also use the eye to follow the videotaped images, but the accompanying words still require the ear. So broadcast news is written for the ear, whereas newspapers are written for the eye. Those who write broadcast news must write clearly and succinctly so that broadcasters can clearly and succinctly read what they have written. The words that pass your lips will pass your listener's ears only once. While the newspaper reader can return to a sentence that might not have made sense upon first reading, no such possibility exists for the hearer of news. Okay, in rare instances they might rewind if they happen to miss something (if they happen to be recording for whatever reason), but for all practical purposes, the words pass the ear only once.

MAKING IT CONVERSATIONAL

And that's why those words must sound conversational. "Sound" is a key word here. True conversation often tends to be an imprecise, start/stop, redundant, rambling kind of exchange. We want to create the feel of conversation without actually copying it. Again, it comes down to the fact that people are listening to what you have written and are now speaking. People are human; they expect you to sound human. And that is why the style of broadcast writing is so important. Style facilitates all those "humanizing" goals of our writing.

Abbreviations

Remember, you, the broadcast reporter, have to read what you have written. Don't set up stumbling blocks to be tripped over. In general, it is easier to read a word that has been written in full rather than its truncated abbreviation. An unfamiliar abbreviation, such as Lt. for Lieutenant or S-F-C for sergeant first class, can be distracting, can cause meanings to be misinterpreted, and can lose the listener who is not familiar with the abbreviation.

Acronyms and Initials

Do use abbreviations both the reader and the audience have come to expect. Generally, people know what you mean when you say F-B-I, C-I-A, N-DOUBLE-A-C-P, or N-C-DOUBLE-A. Use familiar acronyms. Acronyms spell out words made from initials. Use the familiar ones: AIDS, NASA, NOW, MADD, and so on. Do not use hyphens between the letters of an acronym; read them as words.

Addresses

Spell out all names in addresses: avenue, street, highway, place, boulevard, road, and route. Directions that are part of addresses are also spelled out: north, south, east, west. However, the thing to keep uppermost in mind when it comes to addresses is that broadcast news stories rarely include them, unless they are integral to the story. For example, there's no need to tell your audience the exact address of someone charged with bank robbery. Such use of an address is more appropriate to a newspaper story. Time limitations, combined with our goal to sound conversational, dictate this practice.

Ages

Broadcast reports rarely include ages of the people in the story, unless age is germane to the story. For instance, people are interested in how old a person is when he or she dies.

So an obituary profile would naturally include the person's age. People are also interested in unusual angles regarding age. For instance, if a child gets behind the wheel of a car and manages to drive it six blocks without having a wreck, your audience will want to know the child is only six years old. Likewise, if an eighty-year-old man robs a bank, that's unusual because it's not typical of someone that old. But, unlike newspaper writers, TV reporters don't routinely include ages, names, or addresses as a matter of course.

Attribution

Attribution. Say it out loud. Remember it. *Attribution.* Engrave it on your brain. Attribution is the most basic tool of journalism, be it print or broadcast. Reporters are not experts. They gather information and the information they gather is credited to the source, the person from whom the reporter got the information. In broadcast news, the source always comes at the beginning of the sentence: PRESIDENT BUSH SAYS HE WILL BE RE-ELECTED. Bush said it, not the reporter. You want your audience to know that; that's why the attribution comes at the beginning of the sentence, so there will be no mistaking who said what. The surest way for a beginning reporter to become known as an amateur is to omit the attribution. People, your listeners, your viewers, want to know where you got the information. Say it again. Attribution. Remember it. More on attribution in chapter 4.

Dates

Numerals are used for years, whether they begin a sentence or not. Example: 2004 will be an election year. However, spell out dates from the first through the eleventh. After that, the ordinal suffix is used. It's December eleventh, but February 13th. Broadcasters spell out days and months. Separate the day and the year with a comma: Elvis Presley died August 16th, 1977. Again, the idea is to avoid abbreviations or numbers that can confuse.

Fractions and Decimals

Spell out fractions and join them with hyphens: one-fourth, two-thirds, three-eighths.

Spell out decimals one through ten and use hyphens to join them: Eight-point-two, 15-point-seven.

Names

First and last names only are the general rule when writing names for broadcast news. Omit middle names and initials unless a person is well known by his or her middle initial or middle name. Do not use the courtesy titles of "Mr.," "Mrs.," "Mr. and Mrs.," "Miss," or "Ms."

Numbers

Too many numbers confuse people. For listeners, too many numbers in a sentence can start to run together. They can cause the reader of broadcast news to stumble if he or she has to make that quick mental adjustment for a number such as 6,800,000. Instead, you would write: six-million-800-thousand. A better way is to use a qualifying word like almost and round the figure off to almost seven-million. The rule is to round off when possible.

Follow the basic rules for writing out numbers and using numerals. The *AP* (Associated Press) *Broadcast News Handbook* dictates that numbers one through eleven be spelled out. Numerals should be used for 12 through 999. Thereafter, use a combination of numerals and spelling: two-thousand-999. Use hyphens to connect the numerals and spelled-out numbers. Spell out numbers when they begin a sentence.

Ordinals

Spell out ordinals from the first to the eleventh. After that, use the ordinal suffix: 12th, 32nd, 43rd.

Time

Separate a-m and p-m with hyphens. Use a colon to separate hours from minutes: 9:30.

Time is an exception to the rule of numbers. Use the numerals: 10 a-m or 10 this morning.

Symbols

Symbols are not used in broadcast copy. Instead of writing the symbol ($) for dollar, write out the word. Don't write # for number. Don't write & for "and,"or % for percent. The reason is that people read words easier than they can read symbols. Symbols require a quick mental interpretation that can cause the reader to stumble.

Titles

Titles are the exception that prove the rule in writing conversational-sounding copy. Style dictates that the title should come before the name, and some titles do sound conversational when used that way: Mayor Pat Simpson, Dr. Clyde Smith. However, "secretary of human services and welfare Brenda Coleman" is a mouthful. So, whenever possible, we try to shorten titles. One way to handle the long title is to use the title alone on first reference, then in the next sentence use the name only. Listeners will make the connection. Example: THE SECRETARY OF HUMAN SERVICES AND WELFARE SAYS THE SYSTEM NEEDS TO BE OVERHAULED. BRENDA COLEMAN SAYS THE CURRENT SYSTEM IS COSTING

TAXPAYERS TOO MUCH MONEY. Do not use a comma between the title and the name or after the name and the rest of the sentence.

WRITING FOR RHYTHM AND PACE

The rules of style not only facilitate the reading of your stories; they also give your stories rhythm and pace. They are designed to give your spoken words a flow that carries your meaning smoothly, without interference. To this end, broadcasters incorporate the following literary devices:

Active Voice

Broadcast journalists strive to write in the active voice using active verbs rather than in the passive voice using passive verbs. This facilitates writing short, declarative sentences that approximate conversation. A classic example of the active voice you will remember from your earliest English grammar class is the one involving the boy and the ball. *The ball was thrown by the boy* is the passive structuring of that sentence. *The boy threw the ball* is the active version. In the latter sentence the boy begins the action, and so the sentence is stronger, more dynamic. Note also that the passive sentence required seven words while the active voice required only five. As you can see, the active voice results in a much more direct, subject-verb-object sentence structure.

Contractions

People talk in contractions. Do not they? Or *don't* they? Contractions go a long way toward making you sound human when you read your story. That's because we are used to contractions through our everyday conversations. However, just as in conversation, when you want to make a point, dropping the contraction can give your words more impact. Instead of THE PRESIDENT SAYS HE DOESN'T SUPPORT THE SUPREME COURT DECISION, you may want to add emphasis by making it THE PRESIDENT SAYS HE DOES *NOT* SUPPORT THE SUPREME COURT DECISION.

Quotations

Quotations call attention to the fact that you are reading what you've written. You don't want that kind of attention when you are trying to sound conversational. So the writers of broadcast news rarely use direct quotes. The reason for this becomes obvious when you consider the conversational, spoken-word nature of broadcast news. People seldom direct-quote people in everyday conversation. They paraphrase instead. Additionally, there is the risk that the listener will mistake the quoted words for those of the newsperson. However there are those rare times when a quote might be the best option. For instance, if you don't have a sound bite or actuality of a news source saying something that is particularly colorful or telling, you might write something like this: The incumbent characterized his opponent as a, quote, "empty-headed bozo," end quote.

Then there is the technical nature and advantage of broadcast news. In place of quotes, broadcasters use the actual voices of the people involved in the story, the voices they've recorded or videotaped. The actualities or sound bites are the quotes of the broadcast news presentation.

Tense

Broadcast journalists write in the present tense whenever possible. One of the biggest advantages broadcast news has over print is that broadcast news is immediate. This provides for a higher level of interest on the part of listeners. So broadcast journalists use the language of immediacy. That means that instead of writing THE PRESIDENT *SAID* THERE WILL BE NO TAX INCREASE, we make it present tense by writing THE PRESIDENT *SAYS* THERE WILL BE NO TAX INCREASE. We can do that because since the president said there will be no tax increase at the time it was first reported, we can assume he will still *say* it, if asked again, unless or until he changes his mind. So that is what he says about that particular issue. Often the present perfect tense can be used when the present tense won't work. For example, THE GOVERNOR SAYS THE STORM *CAUSED* A BILLION DOLLARS IN DAMAGE can be brought closer to the present by writing THE GOVERNOR SAYS THE STORM *HAS* CAUSED A BILLION DOLLARS IN DAMAGE.

Do not fall into the trap of what critics have termed *TV speak, the false present tense,* or *headline writing* by trying to make something sound immediate that isn't: GOVERNOR SAYS STORM *CAUSES* BILLION DOLLARS IN DAMAGE. Does that sound conversational? Would you say it that way to your mother?

Succinctness

The short, concise declarative sentences written by broadcast news writers contain no more than one complete thought. Any more, and the sentence starts to become unwieldy. Remember, the closer the subject, verb, and object, the less room there is for confusion— on the part of both the reader (you) and your audience.

SUMMARY

Broadcast style is designed to make both the writing and the reading of broadcast copy quicker and easier. It's designed to save time and reduce reader error, or stumbling. Broadcast news reporters have to prerecord their stories under deadline, which means they have to write them not only fast but also in such a manner that they can be recorded as quickly as possible. That doesn't mean reading fast; that means recording them in as few takes as possible. Reporters don't have time to stumble, to start over; they need to get the track recorded because an editor is waiting to put it all together. And, of course, this conciseness becomes even more important when the copy is being read live. Short, succinct, declarative sentences with attention to broadcast style (numbers, abbreviations, title, etc.) make for smooth reading. And it's all done with an understanding that people will be listening.

CHAPTER QUIZ 1

Place a check mark after the correct style usage.

1. The president says _____ said _____ his administration will declare war on crime.

2. The mayor says she will _____ she'll _____ ask the federal government for assistance.

3. The Air Force Lt. _____ lieutenant _____ was found face down in the street.

4. The new sewer system is expected to cost 215,000 _____ 215-thousand _____ dollars.

5. The superintendent says 5% _____ five percent _____ of the money will be used to increase teacher salaries.

6. A-I-Ds _____ AIDS _____ activists say they'll picket the health department if their demands are not met.

7. The new city hall will cost 130-million dollars _____ $130-million _____ .

8. Tom Brill, mayor of Our Town _____ Our Town Mayor Tom Brill _____ says city hall will be closed while the repairs are being made.

9. 18 students _____ Eighteen students _____ have been injured in the accident.

10. The event is scheduled for June first, _____ June 1st, _____ 2003.

CHAPTER QUIZ 2

Select the sentence that correctly uses broadcast style.

1.
   a. "I think everyone should contribute to the homeless," the 34-year-old shelter director said.
   b. The shelter director says everyone should contribute to the homeless.

2.
   a. The city board of aldermen granted the developers of the new sports arena a total tax break of 900-thousand dollars.
   b. The developers of the new sports arena were granted a total tax break of $900,000 by the city board of aldermen.

3.
   a. The stench of 7,000 hogs less than a mile from his house is making his family sick, according to Everett Kennedy, 56, of Quale Creek Rd.
   b. Everett Kennedy says the stench of seven-thousand hogs less than a mile from his home is making his family sick.

4.
   a. Houston Mayor Lee Brown says Tropical Storm Allison has caused an estimated one-billion dollars in damage.
   b. Lee Brown, mayor of Houston, said Tropical Storm Allison caused an estimated 1 billion dollars in damage.

5.
   a. Air Force officials say Lieutenant John Gray was killed when his Phantom Fighter jet crashed into the side of a mountain.
   b. Lt. John Gray was killed when his Phantom Fighter jet crashed into the side of a mountain, according to Air Force officials.

6.
   a. Jill Simpson, an Our Town resident, is one of many who said they were surprised that incumbent mayor Lamar Pat was defeated.
   b. Our Town resident Jill Simpson is one of many residents who say they were surprised that incumbent mayor Lamar Pat was defeated.

7.

    a. Arnold Perrymen, 50, of 1301 Bonnie Dr., was arrested for robbing the East Our Town branch of the First National Bank, according to Our Town Police who charged the suspect.

    b. Our Town Police have charged Arnold Perrymen with the robbery of the East Our Town branch of the First National Bank.

8.

    a. 380 people were killed in the crash.

    b. Three-hundred-80 people were killed in the crash.

9.

    a. At separate meetings, members of the Our Town board of aldermen will be asked to consider approving funding for the basketball arena, which has a projected cost of 50-million dollars, making it by far the most expensive publicly funded building project in the city's history.

    b. The Our Town board of aldermen will be asked to consider approving the funding of the basketball arena at separate meetings. The projected cost of the facility is 50 million dollars. That would make it the most expensive publicly funded building in the city's history.

10.

    a. Fire officials are investigating a fire that destroyed a downtown landmark.

    b. Fire destroyed a downtown landmark last night.

CHAPTER 2

Glossary of Broadcast Terms

SPEAKING THE LANGUAGE

There is no more collaborative work environment than the one you will find in broadcast news. Neither is there a more deadline-oriented field. Therefore, people have to exchange communication quickly and succinctly. Thus, as in most specialized fields, the special language of broadcast news has evolved to expedite quick communication. Over the years, a kind of shorthand has developed to facilitate quick communications between the various members of the news staff, because that deadline is always bearing down on you. Some of these terms are used for both radio and TV.

RADIO NEWS

Those involved in bringing you radio news:
- The news director is in charge of the news department.
- The producer is in charge of the overall newscast.
- The reporter gathers and reports individual stories.
- The anchor reads the news live.

The elements of a broadcast include:
- Actuality: That portion of a tape-recorded interview included in the various stories of a newscast.
- Briefs: Short news stories of about fifteen to twenty seconds for TV, even shorter for radio.

- Bulletin: Urgent, breaking news.
- Copy: The typed news story from which the anchor or reporter reads.
- Dateline: The geographic location from which a story originates (mainly used by wire services).
- In cue: The first three or four words of an actuality used for script direction.
- Kicker: A story that comes at the end of a news section or the end of the newscast.
- Lead: The sentences the anchor reads that set up the news story to come.
- Lead-in: The sentence that sets up or introduces the actuality.
- Natural (or nat) sound: The background sound that gives a story its ambience.
- Out cue: The final three or four words of an actuality used for script direction.
- Package: A self-contained, tape-recorded news story that includes the voices of those interviewed (the actualities) and the voice of the reporter.
- Slug: A brief one- or two-word description of the story usually placed in the upper left corner of the copy so the producer will know at a glance what the story is about.
- Talent: On-air people.
- Track: The reporter's recorded narration.
- Voicer: A report that is narrated by the reporter rather than the anchor.
- Wraparound: The reporter's voice, usually live, wrapped around actualities.

TV NEWS

In TV news:
- The news director is in charge of the news department.
- The executive news producer oversees the total presentation of the daily newscasts.
- The producer is responsible for the hands-on production (structuring and writing) of the newscasts.
- The assignment editor assigns stories to reporters and photographers, monitors police scanners, and dispatches crews to breaking stories.
- Reporters gather and write stories for newscasts.
- Photographers shoot stories for newscasts.
- Editors edit the videotaped reports for newscasts.
- Anchors host the newscast.

The elements of a TV news broadcast include:

- Anchor lead: The introductory portion of a reporter's script that the news anchor reads live on the air in introducing the reporter's story.
- Axis line: An imaginary line that establishes camera direction when shooting a continuity sequence.
- B-roll: A holdover from early TV news when film was used instead of videotape. It referred to the illustrative portion of the film that was to be played on the B-roll projector, with the interviews played back on the A-roll projector. It now refers to the videotape that videographers shoot to illustrate TV news reports.
- Bite: See sound bite.
- Close-up (CU) shot: Concentrates the viewer's attention on a specific area such as the face.
- Continuity editing: Giving the video sequence a natural flow without jumps in place or time.
- Cut: One shot is edited to another with no effects involved.
- Cutaway shot: A shot of something else related to the main action that is being shown.
- Establishing shot: Establishes the location of a shot, where objects are in relation to each other.
- Head-and-shoulders shot: The video framing of the interviewee that includes the head and shoulders only.
- Headroom: The space between the top of the person's head and the top frame of the shot.
- Jump shot: Unnatural movement of people or things within a scene.
- Lead space: The space between the interviewee and the frame of the shot toward which the interviewee looks, either left or right.
- Medium shot: Between an establishing shot and a close-up. In a medium shot people are usually shown from the waist up.
- Over-the-shoulder shot: The interviewee is framed over the reporter's shoulder as the interview is conducted.
- Package: A self-contained report that includes the recorded narration of the reporter and the recorded excerpts of interviews with the people featured in the news story.
- Pan: When the shot sweeps from left to right or vice versa.
- Reader: News copy that the anchor reads on camera without illustrative video.

- SOT: Stands for "sound on tape" and refers to the recorded image and voice of an interviewee simultaneously recorded to videotape. Also known as a sound bite.
- Sound bite: The excerpted portion of a videotaped interview.
- Stand-up: The place within a reporter's package where he or she appears on camera and addresses the audience directly.
- Super: The electronic writing that appears on the TV screen below the head-and-shoulders shot of the person talking in the sound bite. Also called a c.g. or chyron.
- Talking head: Another name for a sound bite or SOT.
- Tilt: When the camera shot moves vertically up or down.
- Voiceover: The voice of the anchor as he or she reads news copy over videotape.
- VO: Short for "voiceover."
- VO/SOT: Short for "voiceover/sound on tape." The anchor reads the copy over videotape that leads into a sound bite or SOT.
- Zoom: The camera remains stationary as the lens moves physically or electronically closer to the subject.

SUMMARY

Broadcast journalists use a specific language to communicate. As time is always at a premium in broadcast news, this language helps speed up the communications process.

CHAPTER QUIZ 1

1. A talking head is another name for the _____ .

2. The excerpted portion of a recorded radio interview is called an _____ .

3. The excerpted portion of a recorded TV interview is called a _____ .

4. SOT stands for _____ .

5. VO stands for _____ .

6. VO/SOT stands for _____ .

7. A self-contained report that includes the recorded narration of the reporter and the recorded excerpts of interviews with the people featured in the news story is known as a _____ .

8. The place within a reporter's package where he or she appears on camera and addresses the audience directly is known as a _____ .

9. The electronic writing that appears on the TV screen below the head-and-shoulders shot of the person talking in the sound bite is called a _____ .

10. A standard part of the TV interview sequence in which the interviewee is framed over the shoulder of the reporter before the shot cuts to the talking head of the person being interviewed is known as the _____ shot.

CHAPTER QUIZ 2

1. The _____ is the first three or four words of an actuality or sound bite used for script direction and editing.

2. A _____ is the reporter's voice, usually live, wrapped around actualities.

3. The story _____ is a brief one- or two-word description of the story, usually placed in the upper left corner of the copy so the producer will know at a glance what the story is about.

4. The reporter's recorded narration is called a _____ .

5. A story that comes at the end of a news section or the end of the newscast is called a _____ .

6. On-air people are called _____ .

7. The _____ is the final three or four words of an actuality used for script direction.

8. A report that is narrated by the reporter rather than the anchor is called a

   _____ .

9. The background sound that gives a story its ambience is known as _____ sound.

10. Broadcast newspeople use the above terms to _____ communication.

CHAPTER 3

The People-izing Concept

THE THEORY OF PEOPLE-IZING

This text is based on the premise that people are interested in people. If you can't buy that premise, you'd probably best find another field in which to excel. The title of this book includes the word "storytelling" because, as any news director will tell you, that's what a good reporter does—tell stories. And to whom does that reporter tell his or her stories? People. Every aspect of radio and TV reporting that we will cover in this book will come back to one thing—people.

The human equation is at the heart of every news story. It begins with the fact that you as the news writer assume that people will be interested in the story you are going to tell. What other audience do you have? Machines? Animals? No, only people are interested in news stories. And when you strip all our concerns down, what in fact are we concerned about most? People. We are preoccupied with people. If we're concerned about unemployment, why are we concerned? Because we are, to a large degree, defined by the jobs we do. We don't want to look like less of a person in the eyes of those around us should we lose our jobs. If we have a family, we have the additional worry of how we'll provide for the financial needs of the people in our family. If we're following an election, we're concerned about the right person for the office, because "we the people" need a worthy leader. If the lead story of the newscast is a murder, we watch because a person was killed. If an animal is tortured and killed, we wonder how a person could do such a thing.

So how is it done? How do I as someone just learning to write journalism put the human equation in my radio report for my broadcast newswriting and reporting class? In my TV report for my TV-reporting class? The answer is simple, if you remember that a *people-ized* story, a human story, always contains at least, and preferably only, one "real" person affected by the story and, in most cases, at least one official. There may be occasions when more than one real person is necessary, but using more than one person affected by the story often has the effect of diffusing the human equation. If the real person you've chosen for your story is the best one, stay with that person; you don't have time to flesh out multiple real people. The sooner you tie your story to a "real" person, the sooner you have your audience's attention, and the more likely you are to define a logical story structure.

Definition of a Real Person

A "real" person is one who has personal experience with the larger story you are telling. That person might be a housewife, a cub scout, a janitor, or a taxpayer. The real person's story is the smaller story that serves to illustrate or humanize the larger story. He or she speaks from a personal perspective.

Definition of an Official

An official is the person you interview for the overview of your story. That person might be the sheriff, a city councilperson, a store owner, or a spokesperson for the tobacco industry. He or she speaks from an official perspective.

Treatment of a Real Person

In order for us, the listeners/viewers, to appreciate your real person's story, we need to know personal information about him or her. A written setup is required. This puts flesh on your real person. So you ask personal questions of your real person, to get those personal responses that give dimension to your real person and, as a consequence, life to your story. For instance, you might ask the age of the person, how many children are in the family, or how long he or she has lived in a particular neighborhood. Use of such information within the story, of course, depends on its relevance to the overall story. These questions are in addition to the questions that directly involve the news event itself. When asking those questions, your aim is to find out how the event affects your real person only.

Treatment of an Official

Because an official speaks from an official capacity, we as viewers/listeners need know nothing about the personal life of the official. Consequently, an official usually needs little or no written setup. Remember, your official is addressing the overall story from an impersonal point of view. In radio, the name and title in a sentence setting up the official's actuality would suffice. In TV, even the name and title could be dropped from the reporter's narrative in favor of an electronic super of that information.

SETTING UP THE REAL PERSON

A Case History

Say you're doing a story on what casino gambling has meant to the economy of Tunica, Mississippi, a year after gambling was legalized there. Your real person would be a Tunica resident who now works for one of the casinos. So you might set up your real person this way: TUNICA RESIDENT WILMA JONES HAD BEEN UNEMPLOYED FOR MORE THAN THREE YEARS. THE 23-YEAR-OLD MOTHER OF TWO WAS BEGINNING TO DOUBT SHE WOULD EVER WORK AGAIN. THAT WAS BEFORE SPLASH CASINO CAME TO TOWN. Now Jones's actuality or sound bite might go something like this: "I was on food stamps; it was tough." Again, her experience reflects the general experience of the residents of Tunica, Mississippi.

Opening Up the Smaller Story to the Larger Story

Because this is not a story about Wilma, but a story about the economy of Tunica after gambling was instituted in that poor county, we must begin to open up the smaller story to the larger story. Example: BUT TODAY WILMA JONES IS ONE OF 15-HUNDRED TUNICA RESIDENTS WHO LEFT THE UNEMPLOYMENT ROLLS TO BECOME PART OF SPLASH'S PAYROLL.

Segueing to Your Official

Remember, your official requires little or no setup; we need to know nothing personal about him or her. So you might go from Wilma to your official like this: THE NEW TUNICA MALL WAS BUILT AS A DIRECT RESULT OF TUNICA'S NEW PROSPERITY. Since we need to know nothing about the official except his name and title, the intro sentence to his actuality could go something like this: MALL MANAGER JIM SMITH SAYS THE MALL WILL SOON BE EXPANDING. Then he starts talking from an impersonal point of view: "We never would have built here if not for the casinos." Time is short in radio, so after the official interview it's time to wrap your report. To keep your report human, you'll probably want to reference your real person again, though you would likely not use another actuality.

You also want to make sure your report is balanced. While things may have improved, there is also likely to be a downside to the story. For instance, you might have found that taxes have increased to pay for increased road use by those out-of-town gamblers taking advantage of this small-town oasis. Your closing might go something like this: BUT TUNICA'S NEW PROSPERITY DOES HAVE A DOWNSIDE. HEAVY TRAFFIC HAS RESULTED IN INCREASED TAXES FOR ROAD MAINTENANCE. HOWEVER, WILMA JONES SAYS THAT DOESN'T BOTHER HER. SHE SAYS NOW SHE CAN AFFORD TO BUY A CAR TO DRIVE ON THOSE ROADS AND PAY HER CITY FEES. CLYDE SMITH, W-X-X-X NEWS.

Putting It All Together

The following is how the body of your story would look in radio script format ("V" stands for the "voice" of the reader):

V: TUNICA RESIDENT WILMA JONES HAD BEEN UNEMPLOYED FOR MORE THAN THREE YEARS. THE 23-YEAR-OLD MOTHER OF TWO WAS BEGINNING TO DOUBT SHE'D EVER WORK AGAIN. THAT WAS BEFORE SPLASH CAME TO TOWN. WILMA JONES NOW WORKS AS A CASINO HOSTESS.

ACTUALITY: Wilma Jones, Casino Hostess
I was on food stamps. It was tough.

V: JONES IS ONE OF 15-HUNDRED TUNICA RESIDENTS WHO LEFT THE UNEMPLOYMENT ROLLS TO BECOME PART OF SPLASH CASINO'S PAYROLL. WITH THE NEW JOBS HAS COME A NEW CONSUMERISM. MALL MANAGER JIM SMITH SAYS THE MALL IS EXPANDING.

ACTUALITY: Jim Smith, Mall Manager
We never would have built here if not for the casinos.

V: BUT TUNICA'S NEW PROSPERITY DOES HAVE A DOWNSIDE. HEAVY TRAFFIC HAS RESULTED IN INCREASED TAXES FOR ROAD MAINTENANCE. HOWEVER, WILMA JONES SAYS THAT DOESN'T BOTHER HER. SHE SAYS NOW SHE CAN AFFORD TO BUY A CAR TO DRIVE ON THOSE ROADS AND TO PAY HER CITY FEES. CLYDE SMITH, W-X-X-X NEWS.

Since this is all new to you, it's likely you didn't notice that this report has an unorthodox structure. It begins with the reporter narrative. The anchor lead is missing. No story, on radio or TV, begins without an anchor lead, and that's the subject of a later chapter.

SUMMARY

Your stories contain two types of interviews. They are (1) the "real person" interview and (2) the "official" interview. The official serves to give your story credibility in that the official helps establish an impersonal overview of the story. Officials are, as a rule, not personally involved in those things upon which they comment. So, in order for your audience to appreciate the overview of your story, they have to have someone with whom to identify, someone who has a more personal connection to the story. All news stories are ultimately about people. People are interested in stories because they are interested in people. The sooner you tie your story to a real person, the sooner you have a story that will interest people. Remember, your story is never about the real person (if a person is the *subject* of your news story, that person would not fulfill the function of a "real person" as defined in this chapter). The real person's story is always the smaller story that serves to illustrate the larger story.

CHAPTER QUIZ 1

Demonstrate your understanding of the people-izing concept with this multiple-choice quiz.

1. People-izing is based on the premise that people are interested in _____ .
   a. people
   b. places
   c. things

2. A real person, according to the premise of this book, is one who has _____ experience with the larger story you are telling.
   a. no
   b. official
   c. personal

3. The real person gives us the _____ story that illustrates the _____ story.
   a. larger
   b. smaller
   c. overview of the

4. In a story about senior citizen volunteers for the local food pantry, which one of the people listed below would you most likely ask for his or her age?
   a. the food pantry director
   b. a person benefiting from the food
   c. a volunteer

5. Which one of the people listed below is least likely to be the real person of your story about a new dress code policy for the high school?
   a. teacher Joe Preston
   b. school superintendent Ann Ritter
   c. student Clyde Phillips

6. Who is most likely to be the real person of your story about a new cancer treatment?

    a. a doctor

    b. a patient

    c. a nurse

7. Which one of these people is most likely to be the real person of your story about a property tax increase?

    a. the tax assessor

    b. a real estate agent

    c. a homeowner

8. Which one of these people is least likely to be the real person of a story about registering for the draft?

    a. the head of the draft board

    b. a parent

    c. an 18-year-old boy

9. Who is most likely to be the real person in a story about a bill to control the sale of handguns?

    a. the president of the NRA

    b. a pawnshop clerk

    c. the legislator who is proposing the bill

10. Who is most likely to be the real person of a story about rising gasoline prices?

    a. a person filling up at a gas pump

    b. a gas station manager

    c. an electric-car salesman

CHAPTER QUIZ 2

Keeping in mind that your official will give you the overview and that you want your real person to respond from a *personal* point of view—his or her own experience of the larger story you are reporting—circle the response most appropriate to a real person.

1. College students responding to a question about the school's new library:
   a. "I think the new library will be good for students because it will give them access to computers and other useful information tools to help them get the most out of the library."
   b. "I'm glad they've finally gotten full-text articles online because it saves me from having to go there in person."

2. Teenagers responding to questions that deal with the issue of teenage drinking:
   a. "I think teenagers drink because they feel insecure, and they don't really know where to get help."
   b. "I was always the designated driver, but usually I'd have a drink or two before the night was over."

3. Responses from participants in a neighborhood watch program:
   a. "I didn't really think about getting involved with the program until my neighbor was shot to death when he surprised a burglar in his house."
   b. "We feel neighborhoods are the first line of defense against crime in our cities, and it's up to each of us to do our part."

4. Responses from women about anorexia:
   a. "I had a friend who just couldn't see how bad she looked. She was just skin and bones, but she thought she looked good."
   b. "I think most women don't think about the consequences; they just want to look slim."

5. Responses from people regarding the issue of gun control:
   a. "I think we all have to do what we can to reduce crime in this country. It's not going to get better by itself."
   b. "Well, if somebody wants to take my gun, he'd better come armed himself."

6. Responses from people regarding the issue of abortion legislation:
   a. I've decided I just can't have a baby at this point in my life; I'm just not ready."
   b. "If the legislation is appealed, it's obvious what the result is going to be—more back-alley abortions and women dying of infections."

7. Responses from bank personnel following a bank robbery:
   a. "He was very efficient. He came in and took a shotgun out of this grocery sack he was carrying and ordered everybody down on the floor."
   b. "Boy, when I saw that shotgun, I just knew we were all dead."

8. Responses from homeowners about raising taxes to fund schools:
   a. "Well, I think they could take those taxes from a sales tax rather than a property tax."
   b. "I don't have kids, so why should I have to pay for schools?"

9. Responses from homeowners about plans to build a homeless shelter in their neighborhood:
   a. "I work forty years to pay off the mortgage on my house and now they tell us they're gonna flood our streets with bums? Over my dead body, they will."
   b. "The community as a whole is against it because it will lower property values across the board."

10. Responses from assembly line workers who are part of a workforce of a thousand who will be laid off by the biggest company in your town:
    a. "Well, of course all of us hate to be leaving, but I'm sure company officials will do what they can to help us."
    b. "What am I gonna do now? There ain't no more factory jobs like this in this town."

CHAPTER 4

Humanizing, Generalizing, and Attribution

DON'T GENERALIZE

Generalizing is a major problem for beginning journalism students. It is a result of the beginner's ignorance of the requirement of attribution. Attribution qualifies, makes clear, and puts statements in proper context. It is attribution that makes our stories specific. Often, a student will disregard this requirement when it comes to putting the real person in context, which results in a story based on generalization.

A Case History

A student wrote a story about a town that was cleaning up after a tornado. She began well enough. Her lead put her actor(s) in action: LOWNDES COUNTY RESIDENTS ARE IN THE PROCESS OF REBUILDING AFTER A DESTRUCTIVE STORM. JANE DOE REPORTS ON HOW THE COMMUNITY IS REACHING OUT TO HELP VICTIMS. But as the story progresses, we hear evidence of only one member of the community helping others of the community. That one person is the real person of the story, but our student reporter generalizes that one real person into all members of the community. Yes, our real person represents all of those people who are helping out, but the story has to give us evidence that others in the community are indeed helping out.

How could our student reporter have made that point and avoided generalizing? By attribution of an official. By asking questions of the disaster official, who could give her the overview of how people are helping people in this community. Instead, in the sound bite she excerpted for her report, the official said: "The agencies that are in town are the Red Cross, Salvation Army, and Golden Triangle Cares Group. They'll be around for months after to help rebuild the whole community." Nothing about how the people of the community are responding, just the agencies that had come to help the people. Had she kept her anchor lead premise in mind and asked specific questions about the people of the community, it's a good bet the official would have responded with anecdotes of his own about people helping people, which our student reporter could have then attributed to him.

A simple question to the Salvation Army official she interviewed might have been phrased this way: Is this person typical of what's happening here? This official would have been in a position to know and would have likely expressed admiration of individual efforts in words similar to these: "I've really been impressed about how selfless people have been. I've seen families sharing what little clothes they have left, blankets and such. Little girls sharing their dollies." That's all the evidence we in the audience need to understand that it's not just this one person, the reporter's real person, who's helping others, but many in the community. Now we have a story with specific evidence we can attribute to an official to support the premise of the reporter's anchor lead.

YOU ARE NOT THE EXPERT

If you begin writing your story with the understanding that almost everything you know about the story you're writing came from someone else, you're more likely to build a solidly structured story, one based on facts gathered through solid reporting, facts that came from someone else. You acknowledge that those facts came from someone else by attributing those facts to that person. That's what attribution is all about.

Attribution is a basic, if not *the* basic, tenet of journalism. Journalists use attribution for the sake of credibility. Attribution not only credits the source; it also gives credibility to the story being reported and to you, the reporter.

Reporters borrow expertise on the subjects they are covering from other people. These people are their sources. Attribution assures viewers these people, these experts, vouch for the information presented in the news. Attribution helps your listeners/viewers understand and appreciate the scope of the reporting that went into producing the story you're telling them.

When starting to write your story, keep in mind that the people who make up your news audience are not interested in your opinion. They've tuned in for the news, not your general observations about the news. They don't consider you to be the expert on the issues of the story you're reporting. If they consider you an expert on anything, it's in the gathering and reporting of the facts that address the issues that make up the news. You're a journalist. The people of your audience will accept that as long as you conduct yourself as a journalist. A person who does not realize the importance and necessity of attribution is not a journalist and does not respect the people who make up his or her audience.

WHEN TO USE ATTRIBUTION

Every time you write a sentence, look at it and ask yourself, Who says? If it turns out you're the one who said it, you should probably drop that sentence because there's a very good chance that you've begun to generalize or editorialize. Every sentence you write should consist of a fact, one that you can attribute to a source. That's not to say the fact should always be attributed. Some facts are givens; they can stand without attribution. We'll get to that.

You only know what people say. If you remember that, you won't be editorializing about your source's state of mind. If the mayor tells you a new road is needed to relieve city traffic, don't substitute the verb "believes" for the attribution "says." You only know what the mayor says. In truth, the mayor could believe she and her brother-in-law, the road contractor, are going to split a ton of taxpayer money as a result of this unnecessary road.

Nowhere is attribution more important than when you are reporting on people in a criminal context. If you are not careful in your attribution, you can inadvertently assume the role of judge and jury. When it comes to criminal activity, if police have made an arrest, you can report that POLICE HAVE ARRESTED MAYOR SUSAN SMITH IN CONNECTION WITH A ROAD-BUILDING SCHEME TO DEFRAUD TAXPAYERS, but be careful that you do not write FOR A ROAD-BUILDING SCHEME TO DEFRAUD TAXPAYERS. Using the word "for" implies guilt, and the mayor could sue your station and you for libel.

If the mayor is charged with official corruption, you can write: MAYOR SUSAN SMITH IS FACING CHARGES OF OFFICIAL CORRUPTION IN CONNECTION WITH A ROAD-BUILDING SCHEME TO DEFRAUD TAXPAYERS, but you would not write FOR A ROAD-BUILDING SCHEME. Again, the word "for" implies guilt, which is for a jury to determine.

In writing stories involving criminal activities, the following phrases can head off libel suits and assure fair treatment of the people of your story: charged with, accused of, and convicted of. Remember, you don't know for sure if a person did the crime or not, even if a jury convicted the person. The relatively new investigative tool of DNA testing has resulted in the release of a number of convicted people from death row.

WHEN TO DROP ATTRIBUTION

When or when not to use attribution can be confusing. Attributing obvious facts in a story not only wastes time but can also make the reporter seem rather naive. As stated earlier, some facts are a given. So, whenever a piece of information is a known, indisputable fact, drop the attribution. If an event is taking place at a certain time, a certain location, or for a certain cost, there's no need to attribute that information. The people of your audience are not going to question whether you made that information up. Why would they? Why would the reporter make it up? If the city library hours are changing, there's no need to attribute that, but the "why" of why the hours are changing should be attributed to the proper official. The "how" of how the hour change might affect the students is a question you would ask the official. His or her answer would warrant an attribution. Why? Because you've asked the question and gotten the official explanations from the source. If nothing else, it shows the scope of your reporting. Could you say the same about the statement that the library is changing its hours? No, because that information was obviously initiated by library officials. You didn't come up with that question; there was no way you could ask questions about changing library hours until library officials announced they were changing hours.

In short, avoid overdoing attribution. If the mayor's secretary says the mayor will hold a news conference tomorrow regarding the proposed new baseball stadium, just say: THE MAYOR WILL HOLD A NEWS CONFERENCE TOMORROW REGARDING THE PROPOSED NEW BASEBALL STADIUM. You don't have to attribute it to the secretary who called to tell you that it's going to happen. It's a matter of verifiable record. It can easily be checked out by any member of your audience who for whatever unfathomable reason may not believe you.

When in doubt about attribution, remember, it basically comes down to two words, one question: Who says? The people to whom you are telling your story will want to know.

THE REPORTER'S OBSERVATIONS

If everything must be attributed, is the reporter ever free to make an observation or draw a conclusion of his or her own?

A Case History

A student reporter covered a story about representatives of *Playboy* magazine visiting the campus to recruit students for the magazine's "Girls of the S-E-C" (Southeastern Conference) issue. During the course of the story we learn, PLAYBOY IS NOT REVEALING WHERE THE INTERVIEWS WITH THE APPLICANTS ARE BEING HELD, THE LOCATION OF THE SHOOTS, OR THE AMOUNT OF MONEY BEING OFFERED. The student prefaced the statement by observing: PLAYBOY IS KEEPING A LOW PROFILE.

After watching the report, several students questioned the reporter's right to make the unattributed "low profile" statement. Did the reporter's statement require attribution? No, it did not. Was it editorializing? No, it was not. Why? Because it was a reasonable and logical consequence of the reporter's own observations. Just as the reporter could state without attribution that city hall burned to the ground if she had witnessed it, she could say *Playboy* was keeping a low profile, because she had witnessed it.

SUMMARY

Attribution establishes the story's reliability and your credibility. It is a means of avoiding two deadly sins that beginning journalism students commit on a recurring basis—editorializing and generalizing. Keep in mind that the people of your audience aren't interested in your opinion and don't consider you the expert on the story. Remember, unless you know who says so, and can name a source other than yourself, you should probably cut that statement from your story, unless it's an independently verifiable fact that no reasonable person is likely to question. On the legal side, attribution could save both you and your station from being sued for libel.

CHAPTER QUIZ

Place an "X" by the following sentences that need attribution, and an "O" by those that don't.

Before making your choice, ask yourself, How do I know this, and is the fact one that is easily verifiable from another source or one likely to be questioned?

_____ 1. Gasoline prices now average a dollar–47 nationwide compared with a dollar–71 last month.

_____ 2. Local gasoline prices have been going down for six weeks straight.

_____ 3. President Bush met with the leaders of both the House and the Senate to discuss his tax plan.

_____ 4. World oil inventories are adequate in spite of Iraq's suspension of its crude exports.

_____ 5. Members of a new task force met for the first time this week to help set a course for the future of the state's forestry industry.

_____ 6. First American Bank in Our Town has its first A-T-M up and running after eight years in business.

_____ 7. Bans on drivers using handheld cell phones have been proposed in 40 states.

_____ 8. When Mayor Lamar Pat presents his budget to the City Council today, there will be at least two major bits of good news.

_____ 9. Though the budget has yet to be presented, there will be no tax increase for property owners.

_____ 10. Union Avenue should stay as it is with no rush hour lane changes.

⟿ CHAPTER 5 ⟿
People and Ethics

DO UNTO OTHERS

In the 1957 movie *Jailhouse Rock*, Elvis Presley shared a cell with a hard-bitten, cynical inmate whose motto was, "Do unto others as they would do unto you—only do it first." Intentionally or not, he had that Biblical injunction just a bit wrong. The actual wording is "Do unto others as you would have them do unto you." In its correct form, that's a pretty good motto for a journalist to live by.

A Case History

A student was doing a story about possible health problems of animals adopted out by the Our Town animal shelter. A friend's puppy had developed a serious infection shortly after being adopted. The student reporter interviewed shelter officials and handed in a rough draft for the instructor's input. The anchor lead read: IF YOU'RE CONSIDERING ADOPTING A PET FROM THE OUR TOWN ANIMAL SHELTER, YOU MIGHT WANT TO THINK TWICE. AS HOPE WALKER REPORTS, YOU COULD BE GETTING A SICK ANIMAL.

While that may have been an accurate assessment of the information in the story to come, it was unduly sensational. As the instructor learned after talking with the student, she'd actually spent a sleepless night worrying about her lead and the tone of her report. Though it seemed accurate enough, she said, it just didn't seem fair. The student possessed what all good journalists must possess—a conscience. She rewrote her anchor lead accordingly: IF YOU'RE LOOKING TO ADOPT A PET, THE OUR TOWN ANIMAL SHELTER HAS A NUMBER TO

CHOOSE FROM. BUT AS HOPE WALKER REPORTS, THERE ARE THINGS YOU SHOULD KNOW REGARDING THE HEALTH OF ADOPTED ANIMALS. The accusatory tone was dropped. The student reporter could sleep again.

LEGAL VERSUS ETHICAL CONSIDERATIONS

In the preceding case history, the student's own sense of right and wrong, or her inner moral compass, served to point her in the right direction. In fact, the student's sense of fair play could well have headed off possible legal ramifications, as shelter officials could conceivably have sued for libel if the original lead had been aired. As journalists, we should always be concerned that our stories avoid unfairly injuring someone with defamatory information. Unfortunately, we sometimes need other guidance in doing the right thing. Consequently, legal standards have been established to protect society from unethical conduct. The following legal and ethical concerns are designed to address conduct that does not conform to accepted standards of right and wrong, specifically as they relate to the practice of journalism. Defamation is concerned with two basic legal issues: libel and invasion of privacy.

LIBEL

As a broadcast journalist, you must always be on guard against the possibility of libel in both your writing and your illustrative video. The courts define libel as published defamation that damages a person's reputation. Therefore, identification of the person must be clear, the libelous material must be published or broadcast, and the resulting report proven to be the consequence of negligence or malice in order for a plaintiff to prevail. Those concerns apply to both our words and our images.

A Case History

A TV reporter was doing a story on a new court ruling regarding pornography. His real person was the manager of a magazine stand. This particular shop sold both mainstream magazines and those magazines that could be termed pornographic. In the background of the interview with the store manager, a customer could clearly be seen thumbing through a magazine whose cover was not visible. Since this was a story about porno magazines, could a reasonable person draw the conclusion that the identifiable man in the background was reading such a magazine? Lawyers for the TV station that broadcast the news report thought so and settled out of court with the lawyer of the man in the background. Yes, that man's reputation stood to be damaged by the reporter's, and hence the station's, negligence.

INVASION OF PRIVACY

Invasion of privacy involves a story that is true, that identifies, and that harms. To defend against a charge of invasion of privacy, the journalist has to prove the newsworthiness of the story.

A Case History

A student reporting team decided to do a story about alcohol and swimming. The student photographer knew someone who had a friend who had broken her neck by diving into the shallow end of an apartment complex pool after a night of drinking. The person had survived, but was paralyzed. The victim was not suing the apartment complex for any wrongdoing, so there was no court case or court decision to make the incident a matter of public record. If a story were done about this accident, could the reporter prove the newsworthiness of the material, or would it amount to an invasion of the victim's privacy? The accident that happened to the particular victim is a private matter and not in itself newsworthy. But the fact that such accidents happen *is* newsworthy.

The reporting student was aware that at least three similar accidents had happened in Our Town over the past couple of years. So there was a definite story there. Unfortunately the student did not consider the privacy issue when trying to broaden the story. He did not attempt to talk to the victim, but instead, in his report, allowed a witness to the accident to name the victim and say that the victim had been drinking and did not follow the rules about diving. Was the report an invasion of privacy? It would have been had it aired. The story would clearly have damaged the victim's reputation.

What if the student reporter had used a friend of the victim as the real person, someone who could talk about the incident, about how it made her feel to see her friend dive into the water perfectly fit and come up paralyzed for life? Would it be okay for the real person to name her friend? No. Would there be a way to do the story ethically, using the friend if she did not name the victim? Yes, but in order to do so, the friend could not be identified either. You'd need to shield her identity along with the victim's. How? By not naming her and by shooting her interview in silhouette. Why not show the friend and just not name the victim? Because that would make identification of the victim possible. In the end, doing the ethical thing, silhouetting the friend, might add to the story because it indicates that no one wants to be identified with such irresponsible behavior as mixing alcohol with swimming.

An ethical, but not legal, issue also comes into play in this story. Was it likely that the victim would want to talk to a reporter about her accident? Given its embarrassing context, not likely, and the reporter should definitely feel hesitant about intruding upon that person's private grief. But should the reporter ask? Yes. You never know—that person may be able to take some solace in sharing her experience with others to help them avoid such risky behavior. Instead of asking the person directly, the issue might be put to a family member. That family member might well see the benefit in sharing the story; and if he or she asked, the victim might agree. The point is that you never know. Such a first-person account would definitely lift the story above the ordinary. But again, the approach to the victim should be extremely tactful.

INVASION OF PHYSICAL SOLITUDE

The ethical debate over the use of hidden microphones and cameras is ongoing among conscientious journalists. It's generally agreed that unless the story is of significant magnitude and there is no other way to gather the facts, the hidden camera and microphone should not be used. People have the right to expect their physical privacy to be respected. Additionally, going onto private property without permission could lead to legal problems.

BALANCE AND FAIRNESS

Reporters who care about people take care to make sure their stories are balanced; that is, they make every effort to fairly present the issues of controversial stories. For example, if you were doing a story on capital punishment, you would want to be sure to get interviews with those for and those against the death penalty. The people watching at home, your audience, would expect no less of you, even if they favored one side of the issue over the other.

SUMMARY

A good journalist has a moral compass. He or she strives to present those pictured in his or her reports in a true, rather than a false, light. The good journalist never operates from a sense of malice, never allows false information to discredit her report. The good journalist plays fair, doing unto others as he would have them do unto him. The good journalist is not likely to have to defend herself in a libel suit.

CHAPTER QUIZ

The following questions are designed to stimulate discussion about legal and ethical choices. Place a check next to the choice you feel is ethically correct, write a brief explanation of your reasoning, and be prepared to discuss it.

1. A minor Our Town city official is killed in a car crash. While gathering some biographical information on him, you discover that he was once charged with child molestation, though the charge was dropped before the case came to trial. That information should _____ should not _____ be included in your story.

2. The execution of Oklahoma bomber Timothy McVeigh should _____ should not _____ have been publicly televised.

3. You do a story about a woman who contracted to have a new roof put on her house. The contractor obviously overcharged her, and the roof still leaks. She has tried to get him to make good on the deal, but he has refused—until you do the story. But before your story can air, the man agrees to fix the roof, but only if the woman can get you to drop the story. You do _____ do not _____ agree to drop the story.

4. A woman stands in front of her house sobbing as firefighters leave after putting out a fire that claimed the lives of her two children. You do _____ do not _____ videotape her, and you do _____ do not _____ try to interview her.

5. You're doing a story about school safety, and a producer suggests that you park outside a school and offer kids a ride home to see if any of them will accept a ride from you, a stranger. You do _____ do not _____ agree that this is a great idea.

6. A movie production company is offering to pay your way to Hollywood to interview the hot young stars of a new film. You do _____ do not _____ accept the offer.

7. You're doing a story about handicap parking and tape a nonhandicapped person returning to her car parked in a handicap spot. You approach her with your camera rolling and ask her why she parked in a handicap spot. She gets really upset, curses you out, and ends up chasing you and your cameraperson across

the parking lot. Later, before your newscast airs, she calls to tell you that if your station airs tape of her, she'll sue. You do _____ do not _____ air the tape.

8. You learn that a local man has been arrested on suspicion of being part of a child pornography ring, but has not been charged. You do _____ do not _____ include the man's name in your story.

9. You learn that the mayor of Our Town has been questioned by police about personally ordering child pornography. He has not been arrested or charged. You do _____ do not _____ report the story.

10. A thirteen-year-old has been charged with murder. The court has ordered that the child not be identified, and officials have been able to shield his identity when taking him to court. However, you've obtained a picture of him from his junior high yearbook. You do _____ do not _____ include his picture and name in your report.

CHAPTER 6

Humanizing the Anchor Lead

THE CONTROVERSIAL ANCHOR LEAD

The anchor lead is often the hardest part of the story for most reporters to write. That's likely why it is also one of the most controversial among newswriting experts. For instance, authors James Julian and Bryon St. Dizier, in the sixth edition of their book, *Writing Assignments for Today's Media*, defend their book's unusually large number of lead-writing exercises by declaring, "You must catch a reader's interest at the beginning of a story with an emotional or informational reward or lose him forever." However, Roy Peter Clark and Don Fry of the esteemed Poynter Institute for Media Studies declare just as adamantly, "Many reporters spend too much time crafting the lead, sometimes as much as half their writing time." They advise "a reporter struggling with leads to think of lead writing as a key part of the process, but not necessarily the first step."

The humanizing approach takes these opposing views into consideration, but while it proceeds from the premise that writing the anchor lead is, indeed, the first step, it provides a formula to lessen the time required to take that first step.

To begin with, think of your anchor lead as your contract with your audience. In it, you promise them a story. In it, you tell them what that story will be. And you do it remembering that they are people interested in people, no matter what the story you are telling, be it social or political, feature news or hard news.

Then think of the people of your anchor lead as the actors of your anchor lead. Every anchor lead contains an actor or actors and a main action.

PUTTING THE ACTORS IN ACTION IN THE ANCHOR LEAD

One of the oldest formulas for deciding how to write a news story is known as the "five Ws"—the who, what, why, when, and where that constitute the structure of a story. There is also an "H" to consider—the "how" of a story. Answer those questions and your story is written. The formula put forth in this book acknowledges those questions, but boils it down to "putting the actor in action." Once you do that, you've answered the "who" and the "what" of the old formula. You can now use that as your guide to fill in the why, when, where, and how.

Finding the actor (the person or persons to propel the story forward) is the quickest way to begin writing the anchor lead, and that's the beginning of the anchor lead formula. While the reporter at the next desk is pulling her hair, spending way too much time thinking about the who, what, why, when, and where—looking for a way to begin her story—you've already begun yours because you've asked yourself, "Who is the actor of this story?" In most instances, that will be the first thing you write down on your blank computer screen. The next part of the formula is to ask yourself, "What is the action?" With the answers to those two questions, you have the first sentence of your anchor lead. Approaching your anchor lead in this manner accomplishes three things—(1) it acknowledges that people are interested in people, (2) it's fast, and (3) it's focused. You know, the producer knows, and the audience knows where your story is going to take them beginning with that first sentence. The second sentence of that anchor lead will also be humanized, as it performs the function of introducing you, the reporter, while more narrowly focusing the story.

PUTTING YOUR ACTORS IN ACTION IN THE PRESENT TENSE

Because both radio and TV are mediums of immediacy, radio and TV reporters write in the present tense. That is a primary concern when you are deciding what the action of your actor is. It should be an action that is happening now.

So now we'll back up and write the anchor lead to our Tunica gambling story. That is, of course, the reverse of what we have just said about the anchor lead, that it should always be written first. We made an exception for the sake of instructional clarity. But the anchor lead to the Tunica gambling story *was* known before the body of the story was written. It had to be in order to structure the story in a satisfying manner. Here is the anchor lead to the Tunica story: THE CITIZENS OF TUNICA COUNTY ARE RIDING THE WHEEL OF FORTUNE INTO THEIR SECOND YEAR OF LEGALIZED GAMBLING. JANE DOE REPORTS ON THE ECONOMIC EFFECT OF GAMBLING ON WHAT WAS ONCE THE POOREST COUNTY IN THE NATION.

To arrive at that anchor lead, the writer asked herself two questions: (1) Who are the actors? and (2) What is the action? Is Wilma Jones the actor? No, again, your story is not about Wilma Jones. The real person of your story is never the actor in the anchor lead. Always remember that the story is not about the real person. The real person's smaller story is always used to illustrate the larger story. So Wilma Jones is not mentioned in the anchor lead because the story is not about how she got a job at the casino, but rather how the town of Tunica is benefiting from the fact that the casinos have come to town. So who is the story about? Who is being affected most by the new legalized gambling, according to your economic approach to the story? Who does Wilma represent? The people of Tunica. The story is about the economic effect of legalized gambling on the people of Tunica.

Now you have your actors, and once you have them, that is the first thing you put down on your blank computer screen: CITIZENS OF TUNICA. Now what is the action? What have they been doing ever since gambling came to town? What are they continuing to do? They're RIDING THE WHEEL OF FORTUNE, and they have been for just over a year at this point. So, remembering that we want our anchor leads to be in the present tense, we don't say the citizens *have* been doing something; we say they *are* doing something: THE CITIZENS OF TUNICA COUNTY ARE RIDING THE WHEEL OF FORTUNE INTO THEIR SECOND YEAR OF LEGALIZED GAMBLING.

Now, the second sentence of the anchor lead is also people-ized, and it logically follows the action of the first sentence with the action of the person, the storyteller who is telling this story, the reporter: JANE DOE REPORTS ON THE ECONOMIC EFFECT OF GAMBLING ON WHAT WAS ONCE THE POOREST COUNTY IN THE NATION. Now when you introduce Wilma in the body of your report, she represents the CITIZENS OF TUNICA, those people of Tunica who have been and are benefiting from legalized gambling in their city.

ANCHORS ARE PEOPLE, TOO

Count the number of words in each of the sentences in the Tunica anchor lead. Notice that each sentence contains twenty words or less. The reason anchor lead sentences should contain an average of twenty words or less is that *people* have to read them. No, your listeners or viewers won't have to read them; the anchor*people* will have to. So remember that anchors are people, too. Anchorpeople need to be able to breathe comfortably as they read. A long sentence requires a long single breath. Also remember that too many words give the anchors too many opportunities to stumble. When sentences are short and direct, they are less likely to be clumsily or awkwardly constructed. When sentences begin with the actors, they are more likely to have a succinct subject-verb-object construction, and that is the best fit for the anchorperson's tongue. This also means the *people* of your audience will be able to clearly understand the story being told. When it comes time to write the body of the story, you will want to follow the same procedure, because you, the reporter, are also a person and you will have to read what you have written.

FOCUSING ON THE ACTOR AND THE ACTION

A Case History

A radio reporting student was given an MIP (minor in possession) citation by the local police. He felt his penalty under a new law was unfair and possibly illegal. The instructor encouraged him to do a report on the issue. The following is the story the student submitted ("ACR" stands for "anchor"):

ACR: THE MISDEMEANOR OFFENSE OF MINOR IN POSSESSION OF ALCOHOL IN OUR TOWN IS NOT AS LENIENT AS IT USED TO BE. AS STEPHEN MALONY REPORTS, A NEW LAW PUTS OFFENDERS ON PROBATION FOR SIX MONTHS, AS WELL AS IMPOSING A STIFF FINE.

V: LOCAL COLLEGE STUDENTS MUST NOW BE CAREFUL IF THEY ARE UNDER-AGE AND ARE CONSUMING ALCOHOL. FRESHMAN DANIEL SHEPPARD SAYS HE HAS RECEIVED A MINOR IN POSSESSION AND WONDERS IF IT'S LEGAL TO PUT HIM ON PROBATION. THE CONDITIONS OF HIS PROBATION ARE THAT HE SUBMITS TO RANDOM DRUG AND ALCOHOL TESTING.

ACTUALITY: Daniel Sheppard, MIP Offender
I got caught drinking a beer and now I get drug tested. I don't get it.

V: THE NEWLY PASSED LAW WENT INTO EFFECT ON SEPTEMBER 15TH AND HAS BEEN ENFORCED VERY STRICTLY SINCE. OUR TOWN POLICE OFFICER T. A. CARTER SAYS HE WRITES ALMOST 30 CITATIONS A WEEK. HE SAYS THE OFFENSES ARE BECOMING MORE AND MORE FREQUENT.

ACTUALITY: T. A. Carter, Our Town Police
I go to The Mill on a Monday night and write out at least seven or eight citations.

V: THE DEBATE ON THE LEGALITY OF THE LAW WILL RAGE ON. THE POLICE SAY THEY WILL KEEP ENFORCING THE LAW WHILE THE STUDENTS SAY THEY WILL KEEP DRINKING. STEPHEN MALONY, W-X-X-X NEWS.

The student had a definite point of view he wanted to express, but it was out of focus because his report contained an obvious editorial bias and was not balanced. Had the student put into practice the formula put forth in class and in this text, he would have begun to look for the focus of his story where? In the anchor lead. Because the first sentence of his anchor lead contains no reference to actors, it's obvious the student did not ask himself who the actors are and what the action is. The instructor knew from talking with the student that the student felt *local police* were overstepping their bounds with the new MIP law. The student told the instructor the new law allowed police to put a minor in possession of alcohol on probation for six months and subject him or her to random drug and alcohol testing during the length of probation. Clearly, on the face of it, there is a valid constitutional question here, one the news media have a right to examine regarding the constitutional protection against illegal search and seizure.

Since it was this action of the police aimed at the student that inspired him to want to do the story, it is equally clear the actors of the story are the police. However, the student's anchor lead did not begin with the police as actors. In fact, the anchor lead contained no actor in the opening sentence and no reference to people at all, only to the law itself. But had the student remembered to *people-ize* his report, it might have opened with something like this: OUR TOWN POLICE ARE NOW PUTTING UNDERAGE DRINKERS ON SIX MONTHS PROBATION AND RANDOMLY TESTING THEM FOR DRUGS. STEPHEN MALONY LOOKS AT THE LEGALITY OF THE NEW MINOR-IN-POSSESSION LAW.

Taking the time to put his actors in action in the anchor lead would have focused the student on what his story was about.

USING THE ANCHOR LEAD TO STRUCTURE THE BODY OF YOUR STORY

Now the student is ready to structure his story around the issue set up in the anchor lead— the legality of the law. Because the student knows the new law has affected *him*, and he wants other students to "NOW BE CAREFUL IF THEY ARE UNDERAGE AND ARE CONSUMING ALCOHOL," what better way, what more logical way, what more bias-free way, than to tell them how many have already been caught under this law? If he's asked the logical question of the right officials, he will have that information when he sits down to write. V: OUR TOWN POLICE SAY THEY'VE ISSUED ABOUT 200 M-I-P CITATIONS SINCE THE NEW LAW WENT INTO EFFECT IN SEPTEMBER.

Now the student can transition to the real person of his story. FRESHMAN DANIEL SHEPPARD WAS ONE OF THOSE CITED. Remembering that he, the reporting student, paid a heavy fine, the student would logically want that to be a part of his story. Again, he would have logically asked his real person what his penalty included: HE SAYS HE WAS FINED 150 DOLLARS AND PUT ON SIX MONTHS' PROBATION FOR POSSESSION OF ALCOHOL. Such detail puts flesh on the bones of your real person.

Now comes the part the student was really interested in—could the police really do that to him in a free country? If his real person hadn't thought of that, he would when and if the student reporter raised the issue by asking the question about being randomly drug tested as part of the probation and asking him if he thought that was legal—again, a valid question in the context of the story. The response would likely have allowed the student to continue as follows: SHEPPARD QUESTIONS THE LEGALITY OF BEING TESTED FOR OTHER DRUGS WHEN HE WAS ONLY ARRESTED FOR POSSESSING ALCOHOL.

The story would then follow with an actuality: Daniel Sheppard, MIP violator. "I got caught drinking a beer and now I get drug tested. I don't get it."

Now, because the only reason the student wanted to do this story in the first place is because he felt the police (the actors set up in the anchor lead) violated his constitutional rights, the student logically needs to talk to someone who knows the Constitution, not a police officer as used in his original story. The best-known advocacy group for the Constitution is the American Civil Liberties Union. There is a chapter in the student's college town: V: A-C-L-U ATTORNEY JIM DOE SAYS THE NEW LAW DOES GIVE HIM CAUSE FOR CONCERN. Then, an actuality: Jim Doe, ACLU: "Unless they have probable cause to suspect you of drugs in addition to the alcohol charge, they are clearly in violation of the Constitution regarding search and seizure."

Now the student has to forget his bias and get the opposing side—this is his chance to ask what he couldn't have very diplomatically asked of the officer while the officer was citing him—is this legal? But the officer who cited him is not the person we would *logically* expect to have the overview. The logical person is the police chief, and our student, in an interview situation, can ask him outright, "What do you say to those who say this new law sounds unconstitutional?" You can bet the chief would have an answer, especially since police don't usually try to enforce a law that hasn't been voted on by the proper governing body after being researched and cleared by the city attorney. In this instance (as determined by the instructor), it turned out the offender has a choice of jail time or conditional probation depending on his or her willingness to submit to random drug tests during the length of probation.

Again, knowing what your story is about, in the anchor lead, gives you the direction you need to write a story that holds together structurally from beginning to end.

USING THE ANCHOR LEAD TO KEEP YOUR STORY ON TRACK

Your anchor lead is a good tool for making sure your story structure holds. If the actuality or sound bite you choose does not refer directly back to your anchor lead, if you can't see the same issue being addressed in your actuality or sound bite as in your anchor lead, it's a strong indication that your story has collapsed or taken an unintentional turn.

Check the preceding revised story and notice how the real person's actuality refers directly to drugs, how the student's "I just don't get it" is directly tied to the question of whether the law is legal.

Check the official actuality: "Unless they have probable cause . . . clearly in violation of the Constitution." Again, the actuality has a direct bearing on the issue raised in the anchor lead.

A Case History

The student videographer and reporter team were doing a follow-up story on town plans following an aborted attempt to establish a historic preservation district. The commission impaneled to come up with the plan had been dissolved following a conflict with property owners.

The two students had kept the instructor informed as they conducted their interviews. By talking with them, the instructor learned that the mayor told them she believed the original proposal had failed because both the property owners and business owners had not been sufficiently "educated" by the original panel regarding what the historic designation could mean to them and their property. The instructor also learned that the administration would try again. From talking to the student reporter and the photographer, he knew who the actors were, what the action was, and where the story was right now.

But when the reporting student turned in her script, the story the instructor expected was nowhere in sight—not in the lead, where it logically had to be. Instead, the first line of the anchor lead gave the instructor (read audience) old news: OUR TOWN PROPERTY OWNERS HAVE HAD A MAJOR PART IN DISSOLVING A HISTORICAL DISTRICT PROPOSAL. Old news. The second sentence did give the new development, "where the story is right now": AS JANE DOE REPORTS, THE OUR TOWN BOARD OF ALDERMEN IS HEADING BACK TO THE DRAWING BOARD TO REWORK PLANS FOR A HISTORICAL DISTRICT. But the context for understanding the follow-up story had already been lost because of the first sentence.

Additionally, the first and second sentences did not go together logically, even if the first sentence had been new news. If the audience is told that PROPERTY OWNERS HAVE HAD A MAJOR PART IN DISSOLVING A HISTORICAL DISTRICT, the expectation is that the next sentence will address that issue. Instead, the student reporter made a common mistake—leaping over, instead of bridging, information. It's the common problem of changing actors in midstream, to adapt an old cliché.

So, again, we begin by asking ourselves who are the actors in this new story that grew out of the old one? In the original story, it was the property owners. Now, it's the city officials' turn. The rewrite: CITY OFFICIALS SAY PROPERTY OWNERS DEFEATED PLANS FOR A HISTORIC DISTRICT BECAUSE THEY DIDN'T UNDERSTAND IT. AS JANE DOE REPORTS, OFFICIALS SAY THEY'LL TRY AGAIN AND GET IT RIGHT THIS TIME. Once the anchor lead is set, it's important to remember it is your road map. Use it as your guide and you won't stray off into uncharted territory.

WHERE IS THE STORY, RIGHT NOW?

We have said that radio and TV news is written in the present tense to give our stories immediacy. To help you remember that, and to make sure you write the most up-to-date anchor lead possible for your story, there is a third question you must ask yourself in addition to the questions, Who is the actor? and What is the action? You must ask yourself, Where is the story, right now? For instance, if three children died in a house fire last night, where is the story right now, today, on your morning newscast? With a little checking you could find out. Most likely, fire officials are still investigating, and most likely funeral arrangements are being made. So, instead of beginning your story with THREE CHILDREN DIED IN A FIRE, your story might begin with FIRE OFFICIALS ARE INVESTIGATING THE CAUSE OF A FIRE THAT TOOK THE LIVES OF THREE CHILDREN, or FUNERAL ARRANGEMENTS ARE BEING MADE FOR THREE OUR TOWN CHILDREN WHO DIED IN A HOUSE FIRE.

Let's refer back to our case history regarding Our Town's historic preservation. If our student reporter had asked herself the question, Where is the story, *right now*? it would have been difficult for her to proceed with the *old* news angle. She would have realized upon writing OUR TOWN PROPERTY OWNERS HAVE HAD A MAJOR PART IN DISSOLVING A HISTORICAL DISTRICT PROPOSAL that the story had advanced from that point. She would have focused instead on the new news of her story: CITY OFFICIALS SAY PROPERTY OWNERS DEFEATED PLANS FOR A HISTORIC DISTRICT BECAUSE THEY DIDN'T UNDERSTAND IT. Then she could have more narrowly focused her lead to the fact that OFFICIALS SAY THEY'LL TRY AGAIN AND GET IT RIGHT THIS TIME (see boxes 6.1 and 6.2).

BOX 6.1   *The Radio Script Format*

ACR: "A-C-R" STANDS FOR ANCHOR, AND THIS IS WHERE YOU PUT YOUR ACTOR IN ACTION. THE ANCHOR LEAD IS ALL CAPS, SINGLE SPACED, AND TWO SENTENCES ONLY.

V: "V" STANDS FOR VOICER. THIS IS WHERE YOU BEGIN WRITING THE PART YOU WILL RECORD. IT IS DOUBLE SPACED, AND IT IS GENERALLY THREE TO FOUR SENTENCES LONG. THE LAST TWO SENTENCES WILL ALWAYS REFER DIRECTLY TO YOUR REAL PERSON, WHO IS ALWAYS YOUR FIRST ACTUALITY.

ACTUALITY: Real person's name, title

This is where you type the excerpted part of your "real person's" recorded interview that you have chosen for your actuality. It is upper- and lowercase and single spaced.

V: THIS IS THE PART OF YOUR REPORTER NARRATION WHERE YOU TRANSITION TO YOUR OFFICIAL. THIS PART IS ALL CAPS, DOUBLE SPACED, AND USUALLY NO MORE THAN TWO TO THREE SENTENCES LONG.

ACTUALITY: Official's name, title

This is the excerpted portion of your official's recorded interview, and it is single spaced and upper- and lowercase.

V: THIS IS THE CLOSING PART OF THE REPORTER NARRATION. IT IS ALL CAPS, DOUBLE SPACED, AND USUALLY ABOUT TWO SENTENCES LONG, EXCLUDING THE LAST SENTENCE. THE LAST SENTENCE CONTAINS YOUR NAME AND THE STATION FOR WHICH YOU WORK— JACK DOE, W-X-X-X NEWS.

BOX 6.2   *The People-ized Package Paradigm*

As reporters, we write packages—self-contained stories featuring common elements—the anchor lead, the real person experience, the official, and the real person conclusion. Think of the package as a box, and think of the common elements as building blocks within the package. Use the blocks to build (structure) your story. The anchor lead is the foundation upon which your story is built, so we start from the ground up.

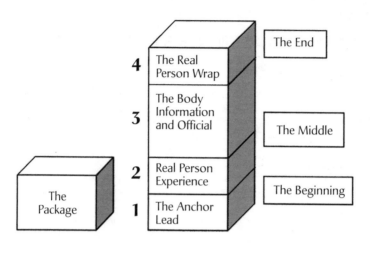

The Package

4 The Real Person Wrap

3 The Body Information and Official

2 Real Person Experience

1 The Anchor Lead

The End

The Middle

The Beginning

SUMMARY

In order to write your story, you must know what it is. The anchor lead is where you discover what your story is. The equation for doing that is found in the answer to these three questions: Who is the actor? What is the action? Where is the story, right now?

CHAPTER QUIZ 1

Demonstrate your understanding of the concept of the humanized anchor lead.

1. What are the two questions you must ask yourself in order to humanize your anchor lead and establish the premise of your story?

2. What third question must you ask yourself to make sure your story is as up to date as it can be?

3. True or false: The real person of your story is always mentioned in your anchor lead.

4. The anchor lead should consist of how many sentences?

5. Anchor lead sentences and the sentences of your stories generally should consist of no more than _____ words.

6. Who is always the actor of your second sentence?

7. In a story about summer school enrollment, who would most likely be the actors of your anchor lead?

8. In a story in which the public is warned by police about a new door-to-door con artist scam, who would you expect to be the actors of your anchor lead?

9. In a story about the findings of government researchers in regard to pesticides, who would most likely be the actors of your anchor lead?

10. In a story about federal assistance being made available to affected homeowners in the aftermath of a flood, who would probably be the actors of your anchor lead?

CHAPTER QUIZ 2

Keeping in mind that a good anchor lead puts the actors in action, choose the anchor lead sentence that best puts this concept in practice.

Anchor lead 1:

    a. THE BODIES OF THREE MISSING CHILDREN HAVE BEEN FOUND BY HUNTERS IN NORTH SHELBY COUNTY.

    b. HUNTERS HAVE FOUND THE BODIES OF THREE MISSING CHILDREN IN NORTH SHELBY COUNTY.

Anchor lead 2:

    a. AN INVESTIGATION IS UNDER WAY INTO THE THEFT OF EMPLOYEE FILES FROM CITY HALL.

    b. POLICE ARE INVESTIGATING THE THEFT OF EMPLOYEE FILES FROM CITY HALL.

Anchor lead 3:

    a. RUSH HOUR MOTORISTS WILL BE DELAYED BY CONSTRUCTION ON HIGHWAY 7 THIS MORNING.

    b. CONSTRUCTION WORK ON HIGHWAY 7 WILL DELAY RUSH HOUR MOTORISTS THIS MORNING.

Anchor lead 4:

    a. A 13TH SUSPECT HAS BEEN ARRESTED IN CONNECTION WITH A PLAN TO BLOW UP THE FEDERAL BUILDING IN ARIZONA.

    b. THE FBI HAS ARRESTED A 13TH SUSPECT IN CONNECTION WITH A PLAN TO BLOW UP THE FEDERAL BUILDING IN ARIZONA.

Anchor lead 5:

    a. CYBERSLEUTHS ARE USING THE INTERNET TO TRACK DOWN MISSING PEOPLE.

    b. THE INTERNET HAS BECOME A FAST WAY TO TRACK DOWN MISSING PEOPLE ACCORDING TO EXPERTS IN THE FIELD.

Anchor lead 6:

a. THE THREAT OF ANOTHER HOLOCAUST WILL BE THE TOPIC OF A SPEECH TO BE DELIVERED TOMORROW BY A SURVIVOR OF WORLD WAR TWO'S GERMAN CONCENTRATION CAMPS.

b. A SURVIVOR OF WORLD WAR TWO'S GERMAN CONCENTRATION CAMPS WILL SPEAK TOMORROW ON THE THREAT OF ANOTHER HOLOCAUST.

Anchor lead 7:

a. A LOCAL MAN IS GOING TO PRISON FOR LIFE FOR THE MURDER OF HIS WIFE.

b. A LIFE SENTENCE HAS BEEN HANDED DOWN TO A LOCAL MAN CON-VICTED OF MURDERING HIS WIFE.

Anchor lead 8:

a. A CITY COUNCIL PROPOSAL TO BAN SMOKING IN PUBLIC EATING ESTAB-LISHMENTS HAS DRAWN OPPOSITION FROM RESTAURANT OWNERS.

b. RESTAURANT OWNERS ARE OPPOSING A CITY COUNCIL PLAN TO BAN SMOKING IN PUBLIC EATING ESTABLISHMENTS.

Anchor lead 9:

a. TORNADOES BATTERED THE MID-SOUTH TODAY, LEAVING HUNDREDS HOMELESS.

b. HUNDREDS OF MID-SOUTHERNERS ARE HOMELESS IN THE WAKE OF OVERNIGHT TORNADOES.

Anchor lead 10:

a. THE MOTHER OF A 13-YEAR-OLD BOY IS GIVING HIM ONE OF HER KIDNEYS.

b. THANKS TO HIS MOTHER, A 13-YEAR-OLD BOY IS GETTING A NEW KIDNEY.

CHAPTER 7

Humanizing the Body of Your Story

IT'S YOUR STORY

Just as there are no two people alike, there are no two reporters alike—which means there are no two stories alike. Make the story your own.

THE REPORTER'S NARRATIVE

"Journalists may occasionally claim they are merely messengers, passing on the facts that come to them, but this pose won't withstand scrutiny. At their most accomplished, journalistic narratives may appear natural and inevitable, as if each story had to be told and could not have been told another way. But the facts are chosen and shaped by journalists," according to Robert Fulford in *The Triumph of Narrative: Storytelling in the Age of Mass Culture*.

The choices are yours to make. The more you know about the elements of your story, the more informed your choices will be. Nothing will happen arbitrarily.

WRITE TO YOUR REAL PERSON

The body, or middle of the story, continues the narrative storyline set up in the anchor lead and contains the essential background and explanation. Because of the time factor, and because we don't want to confuse or distract our audience with too many details, the body of the story contains only those facts necessary to support the story's premise, the one most important idea. It should take, on average, no more than four to five sentences to establish the facts necessary to set up your first sound bite. In order to tell a humanized story, those facts must be tied to the real person as soon as possible. Your narrative will not involve us, your audience, until you've introduced and involved your real person in the story. So begin introducing the real person by the second sentence of the body of your narrative. In rare instances, you may not be able to bring the real person in until the third sentence, but always shoot for the second. Why not the first sentence? Because routinely introducing our real person in the first sentence of the body would give our stories a sameness and predictability we want to avoid. Nothing bores an audience quicker than predictability. If we make sure that first sentence of the body flows *logically* from the anchor and then transitions *logically* to the real person, our audience will be much less likely to question our methods.

PUTTING FLESH ON YOUR REAL PERSON'S BONES

So at least two of those first four or five sentences that begin the body of your reporter narrative should be devoted to setting up your real person. They should immediately precede the real person's actuality or sound bite. Those sentences tell us something personal about the real person before we actually hear from him or her. Let's return to our real person from chapter 3, Wilma Jones of Tunica, who got a job at Splash Casino. The reporter narrative began: TUNICA RESIDENT WILMA JONES HAD BEEN UNEMPLOYED FOR MORE THAN THREE YEARS. THE 23-YEAR-OLD MOTHER OF TWO WAS BEGINNING TO DOUBT SHE'D EVER WORK AGAIN. THAT WAS BEFORE SPLASH CAME TO TOWN. Yes, we began by referencing our real person, but again, if we did that with every story, we would soon set up that unwanted pattern of predictability. So, with that in mind, how might we begin our narrative without referencing Wilma (whom we do expect to transition to as soon as possible)? We might consider using natural sound. What sort of natural sound do you logically expect to hear in a casino? How about the whirring of slot machines? The click of a roulette wheel? Then our first sentence could play off that: THAT'S THE SOUND OF MONEY IN TUNICA, MISSISSIPPI, THESE DAYS. AND IT'S MUSIC TO WILMA JONES'S EARS. Then we would continue our narrative as before.

WRITING TOWARD THE OFFICIAL SOUND BITE

Whether you're in radio or TV, keep in mind that in most instances you should write no more than six or seven sentences before the real person begins to speak—two in the anchor lead, four or five in the body.

Every word you write, beginning with the anchor lead, should take into account the fact that you are writing toward your real person's actuality or sound bite. You should know exactly what the real person is going to say in that first sound bite from the very first moment you begin to write your story. The same is true of the official sound bite or actuality you plan to use. This means you have to know the content of your sound bites before writing the first word of your report. Doing this reinforces the coherency of your narrative from the top down.

CHOOSING THE HUMANIZED ACTUALITY OR SOUND BITE

The voices of your real person and of your official are integral parts of your written narrative. Keep this in mind as you write your narrative, the narrative you will read: no matter how golden and dulcet the tone of your voice, no matter the amount of credibility in your delivery, the longer you go on before bringing in the voices of your real person and official, the more you risk losing the attention of the people in your audience. We are creatures of rhythm; that's why music is such a prevailing force in people's lives.

Your actualities or sound bites are an integral part of the narrative rhythm of your story. They are not simply dropped in because it's about time; they are carefully placed in at the right time. They speak up at the most opportune moment for them to do so because it is the most logical place in the narrative for us, your audience, to hear what your real person or official has to say. Remember, though the words are those of the interviewee, you decide where and when to put them in the story. Similarly, you decide what part of the interview to excerpt for your sound bite or actuality, just as you decided what question to ask that elicited the response that resulted in the original actuality or sound bite.

Make sure the sound bite you select is interesting, that the person is saying it better than you could paraphrase it. Listen for those comments that intrigue you, that interest you; then, trust that your audience will feel the same as you.

TEN SECONDS, ONE THOUGHT

The average sound bite should be no longer than ten seconds and should contain no more than one thought. Even the most articulate person can seem to begin to ramble if you let her or him go on for more than one thought in your sixty-second (for radio) or ninety-second (for TV) production. Keeping the sound bite to one thought keeps the story on course, keeps it focused. More than one thought, and you risk losing the rhythm of the story's narrative.

To the critics who bash the short sound bite, we remind them that the tone and timbre of a person's actual voice can say as much as his or her actual words. We also remind them that one picture of an interviewee in a head-and-shoulders-shot sound bite can be worth a thousand (more) words because we can see their slyness, assuredness, and so on.

USING THE ACTUALITY OR SOUND BITE TO STAY ON TRACK

If the content of the sound bite you have chosen does not refer directly back to your anchor lead, then your story has probably lost its thread and has begun to unravel. Use your sound bite or actuality as a guide to keep your story structure from coming apart. Look at the Tunica example. Note that Wilma's first sound bite is directly related to the economy (her economy). Look at the actuality from the mall manager. Again, his sound bite references the economy. Also note that Wilma's final sound bite again reflects the economic angle of the story.

OPENING UP THE SMALLER STORY TO THE LARGER STORY

Always keep in mind that your story is not about the real person of your story. The real person's story (see the Tunica example) is the smaller story used to illustrate the larger story. So after your real person has spoken in his or her first sound bite, it's time to segue to your official for the overview.

SEGUEING TO YOUR OFFICIAL

Because we normally need to know nothing personal about the official, the segue to the official should usually be no more than two or three sentences. Sometimes just one will do it. In radio, you do have to name the official, or else your audience will have to guess who's talking. However, in TV, words referring directly to the official can usually be dropped in favor of additional story information because the name and title of the official will be supered over the interview shot of the official for your audience to read.

KEEPING IT REAL

Remembering that people are interested in people, we keep our story real by referencing our real person in the reporter's final narrative in our radio report, and by returning to our real person for a final comment before closing out the story in our TV report. Segueing to that last comment in the TV report should usually take no more than one or two sentences. After that sound bite or actuality, the story can usually be wrapped up in a couple of sentences at most.

SUMMARY

Weave sound bites into your narrative. Know what the real person of your story is going to say before you begin writing, and write to your real person from the very first sentence of your anchor lead. Know what it takes to put flesh on the bones of your real person. Involve your audience with your real person. Know what your official is going to say before you begin writing, and write toward that sound bite from the first anchor sentence. The more you know about the elements of your story, the more your story will sound as though it couldn't have been written any other way than the way you wrote it.

CHAPTER QUIZ

1. On average, excluding the anchor lead, you should write no more than
   _____ to _____ sentences before the voice of your first sound bite or
   actuality begins.

2. You should begin introducing your real person into the body of your story by the
   _____ sentence, at the earliest, and by the _____ sentence, at the latest.

3. True or false: You should begin writing toward your real person's sound bite in
   the anchor lead's first sentence.

4. True or false: You should begin the body of your report by introducing your real
   person in the very first sentence.

5. True or false: Your overall story is never about the real person.

6. The average sound bite should be no more than _____ seconds.

7. The average sound bite should contain no more than _____ thought(s).

8. The transition to your official should take, on average, no more than _____
   sentences.

9. Your sound bites should always relate directly back to the _____ in order
   to make sure your story stays on track.

10. Try to select sound bites in which the person is saying it better than you could
    _____ it.

CHAPTER 8

The Humanized Interview

JOURNALISTS ARE PEOPLE, TOO

"Being interviewed is a terrible experience," says William Glaberson of the *New York Times* in an interview with Chip Rowe in the *American Journalism Review's* NewsLink, May 28, 2000. "I do sometimes wonder why people subject themselves to it." The answer is simple, in the view of this book: it's because they are people.

Rowe's article was about the reaction of journalists when the tables are turned—when they are the ones being interviewed. Most don't like it, and yet Rowe managed to interview them about their views on being interviewed. That's because journalists are people, too, and like most people they like to talk. According to Ken Metzler, in his book *Creative Interviewing*, reporters estimate that 75 to 80 percent of their information is gathered through interviews.

ACHIEVING FOCUS VIA THE HUMANIZED INTERVIEW

The actuality (radio) or sound bite (TV) can make or break your story. In order to lift just the right ten-second (or so) excerpt from your recorded interview, you have to ask the kind of questions that will elicit significant detail, which often includes the emotional reaction to your questions, especially when you ask those questions of your real person that evoke personal responses of passion and feeling. You must be interested enough, curious enough about people to ask questions that will give both relevance and life to your story.

A good reporter (no matter how experienced) always has a list of questions written out before setting out to do an interview. This is necessary for interviewing not only your official but also your real person. This means you must think about your story before conducting the interview, or even making the phone call to set up the interview. You must have an idea about what the story is about. For instance, if you're doing the Tunica gambling story, what aspect of gambling are you covering? Crime? Religious opposition? The effect on the economy? Pollution? If you decide it's about the economy, prepare by writing out two sets of questions—one set to ask your real person and one set to ask your official.

Whom should you interview first, the real person or the official? It probably won't make that much difference. If you interview the official first, you may have a better idea of what to ask your real person because now you have a better overview of the story. Having the overview, you can fashion real-person questions relating to specific areas central to the story. However, if you interview the real person first, you may discover some insights from the grassroots level that will give you questions to ask of the official you might not have considered otherwise. Either way, you can always do follow-up phone calls for answers to any questions that may occur after your on-scene interviews.

QUESTIONS FOR THE OFFICIAL

Remember, your list of questions for your official is, with few exceptions, impersonal.

1. What problems have been caused by the increased traffic?
2. What effect has all this development had on city services such as city fees, garbage pickup, road maintenance, and police coverage?
3. How much has the overall tax base increased?
4. How have things changed in Tunica now that more people are working?
5. Are there any big development plans?
6. Are any new schools being constructed?
7. Have any new city workers been hired?

When these questions are answered, you have the impersonal overview of the story. Now, for your real person interview. Remember, all of the questions you ask of your real person must be personal. So, if you're doing the Tunica economy story, you make a list of questions to ask of your real person that are economy related, even before you find that casino employee or know that Wilma Jones is going to be your real person.

QUESTIONS FOR THE REAL PERSON

Those questions would likely include the following:

1. What was *your* life like before *you* got the job at Splash?
2. How has *your* life changed since *you* got the job?
3. Fees for city services have gone up. How has that affected *you*?
4. Give me an idea of what *you've* been able to do since *you* have had a steady income from a steady job.
5. Did *you* get a new car?
6. What about *your* kids—what have *you* been able to do for them?
7. Does it give *you* a sense of independence? How so?

Again, all your questions are about her while at the same time they are focused on the overall story of the economy. In addition, and most likely not part of the recorded interview in which you hope to find your actualities, you would ask if she has children, how many, their ages, how long she's lived in Tunica, and so on. These kinds of questions are mainly for you to use in your narrative setting up the sound bite, which will consist of more significant detail.

RECOGNIZING THE NUGGETS IN YOUR INTERVIEWS

When interviewing, try not to hang on to any preconceived notions of what your story is about. Be prepared to go where the story leads you.

A Case History

A reporting student was doing a story on Halloween pranks the day after Halloween. The officer he interviewed told the student it was a pretty quiet night in the small college town—no complaining phone calls from residents about property damage—and he said that was typical of Halloween in this particular small town. The student continued to ask questions of the officer and turned up some interesting and conflicting information. But the student ignored it. His anchor lead read: HALLOWEEN PRANKSTERS ARE NOT A MAJOR CONCERN FOR OUR TOWN RESIDENTS. The student was obviously buying into that old adage, "No news is good news": there's nothing to worry about in our town. Having convinced himself in his anchor lead that he had no story, the student then began to grasp for things to tell his audience as he began his reporter narrative about his nonstory.

V: WEBSTER'S DICTIONARY DEFINES PRANKING AS ANY MALICIOUS ACT. LAST HALLOWEEN NIGHT POLICE HAD NO CALLS FOR INCIDENTS OF PRANKING. A LOCAL RESIDENT SAYS IT'S NICE NOT TO HAVE A PROBLEM WITH PRANKSTERS. AARON MADSON SAYS HE DOESN'T WORRY ABOUT HIS THINGS GETTING DESTROYED.

ACTUALITY: Aaron Madson, Our Town resident
As long as nobody's throwing pumpkins off the overpasses, the kids should have a little fun.

V: PRANKING COMES UNDER THE MALICIOUS MISCHIEF STATUTE. IF FOUND GUILTY, THERE COULD BE A FINE OF TWICE THE VALUE OF THE PROPERTY DESTROYED AND UP TO 12 MONTHS IN JAIL. POLICE SAY OUR TOWN DOESN'T HAVE MUCH MALICIOUS DAMAGE. POLICE CHIEF JOHN POPERNIK SAYS PRANKING TYPICALLY ONLY INCLUDES EGGING AND TOILET PAPERING.

ACTUALITY: John Popernik, Police Chief
We have not had an occasion where we had any really destructive situation.

V: DESPITE THE FACT THERE WERE NO PRANKS ON HALLOWEEN, POLICE WILL CONTINUE TO MAKE SURE THINGS DON'T GET OUT OF HAND. JOHN DOE, W-U-M-S NEWS.

A good indication that the student had no story was his reverting to the theme paper approach in his first sentence: WEBSTER'S DICTIONARY DEFINES . . . Had he truly thought about the difference in definitions of "prank" as stated in the dictionary and as defined by the officer he talked to, the student would have realized that there is a big difference as far as the cop was concerned between a "prank" and "malicious mischief." The instructor realized this when he listened to the entire interview the student had done with the officer. Had the student listened to what the officer was saying, he might have started thinking about a story that would truly interest his audience. The cop clearly thought of toilet papering yards as a prank. To him, and consequently to the law, rolling yards (toilet papering) was a prank, not malicious mischief, and he told the student reporter the police generally looked the other way in such instances.

As the interview continued, the officer talked about how the local cops viewed Halloween tricks—rolling yards was a prank, he said, "mostly done by little girls," and that didn't normally result in a charge. He went on to say that he was "flabbergasted when I walked into Wal-Mart and saw all the toilet paper gone. Just empty boxes where the toilet paper rolls had been." What did that comment reveal? It revealed that Halloween night in this small town was indeed a night for pranksters. Police may not have received any phone calls from irate property owners, but obviously the cops had reason to believe a lot of yard rolling went on this Halloween. In fact, before the story was done, the students and I had discussed the fact that the railroad overpass over the city's major street had been rolled, streamers falling down to be swept onto the street by the first car through the underpass. Considering that his story's real person's comment was, "As long as they're not throwing pumpkins off the overpass, I don't see any problem with kids having a little fun," the reference to the rolling of the overpass would have made a great, logical way of getting into a story about Halloween pranks.

But the student reporter either was not listening, or he ignored the distinction the officer made about harmless pranks and malicious mischief. The officer went on to make clear the types of incidents he considered malicious mischief, specifically citing egging and paintballing, and making it clear they had happened in the past. He went on to specify the punishment for such actions. The student not only ignored the officer's serious distinction but went on to erroneously equate egging with harmless yard rolling in his story.

Had the student listened to the officer, the student would have begun to see a story that put Halloween in his small town into perspective for his listeners. First he would have asked himself, "Who are the actors of my story?" His choices would have been the police or the pranksters or even the employees of Wal-Mart, which would be a logical way to write the story in the present tense: WAL-MART EMPLOYEES ARE RESTOCKING THE SHELVES WITH TOILET PAPER TODAY, AFTER A NIGHT OF YARD ROLLING BY HALLOWEEN PRANKSTERS. AS JOHN DOE REPORTS, POLICE DON'T MIND YARD ROLLERS, BUT DON'T EGG THEM ON. Okay, so it's a little cute, but it definitely sets up a story, in fact, the story to come, as any good anchor lead should.

How might such a story have continued? A couple of ways come to mind. To begin with, is there one of you reading this who hasn't rolled a yard or had your yard rolled? Rolling yards is part of our universal consciousness. So why couldn't your story begin this way, following your anchor lead: EVER HAD YOUR YARD ROLLED? DID YOU LAUGH IT OFF OR DID IT MAKE YOU MAD? Now, let's transition to our real person, of whom we've already asked those questions: RESIDENT AARON MADSON SAYS HE'S NOT ONLY HAD HIS YARD ROLLED, BUT ROLLED A FEW HIMSELF. HE SAYS IT'S PRETTY HARMLESS.

Then, you could use an actuality from Aaron Madson, Our Town resident: "As long as nobody was throwing pumpkins off the overpasses."

And didn't our student find that the local cops pretty much agreed with that? So he could transition to the official: LOCAL POLICE PRETTY MUCH AGREE, AND THEY HAVE REASON TO BELIEVE MOST RESIDENTS DO TOO. POLICE RECEIVED NO COMPLAINTS FROM IRATE HOMEOWNERS—EVEN THOUGH POLICE CHIEF JOHN POPERNIK SAYS THERE'S GOOD EVIDENCE A LOT OF YARD ROLLING WENT ON.

Now the actuality from Lieutenant Popernik: "I was flabbergasted when I walked into Wal-Mart and saw all the toilet paper gone."

Now we have information that lends substance to our wrap-up:

> V: POPERNIK SAYS ROLLING YARDS IS CONSIDERED A PRANK AND DOESN'T USUALLY RESULT IN A CHARGE. BUT HE SAYS OTHER HALLOWEEN TRICKS LIKE EGGING AND PAINTBALLING ARE CONSIDERED MALICIOUS MISCHIEF. THEY COULD RESULT IN A FINE AND UP TO A YEAR IN JAIL. JOHN DOE, W-U-M-S NEWS.

Notice how including the logical facts changes the editorial ending of the student's original report: POLICE WILL CONTINUE TO MAKE SURE THINGS DON'T GET OUT OF HAND. It is not the reporter's job to predict the future, and it's certainly not the reporter's job to act as a public relations flack for the police department.

The student did an excellent job of interviewing the officer. Police officers are seldom very talkative when it comes to being interviewed by reporters. However, this student had the officer talking so much that he said things he might have regretted later on, for instance, his comment about looking the other way when yards are rolled. On the taped interview, it was obvious the student was enjoying the conversation with the officer, and the officer obviously felt that. The student also presented no threat, in that he often interjected agreement with what the officer was saying. This is not to condone journalists interjecting their personal feelings into an interview, especially not indications of agreement. However, the more conversational you can make your interview, the better. What this student's interview does make clear is that no matter how good the interview might be, if the reporter is not listening for a story, he or she can miss it.

Remember, when you are asking questions, you are asking them for your audience. You're asking the questions they would ask if given the opportunity. Don't miss the story. Listen to the interviewee. Listen for those golden nuggets of sound.

DO YOUR INTERVIEW HOMEWORK

A Case History

A TV reporting student was doing a story on the removal of asbestos from the exterior windows of the building in which the student attended classes and even worked as part of the student media staff. When he talked with the university official responsible for contracting for the asbestos removal, the official told the student reporter that the school wasn't interested in removing asbestos as much as it was in painting the windows. He explained to the student that in order to paint the windows, the asbestos had to be removed. Said the official, "They're going to repaint the windows, that's the main project over there, is painting, so they're removing some of the old putty that contained a small amount of asbestos."

The official succeeded in making the student think the asbestos really wasn't worth considering, even though the student had seen the yellow tape put up by a hazardous materials crew, warning students and others not to pass beyond that point. In fact, the TV-reporting student did his stand-up in front of the yellow tape and rather naively said: HALE SAYS THERE'S NO NEED FOR PASSERSBY TO BE WORRIED—HEALTH RISKS ARE MINIMAL . . . AS LONG AS YOU DON'T CROSS THIS LINE. That drew quite a laugh from his fellow students during the critique session. Had the student been listening to the conversation around the building during the time the asbestos was being removed, he would have heard people joking about how sure they were that the "crime scene" tape was going to keep those airborne particles in their place, behind the line and out of the air. No way were those particles going to blow across the campus!

Had the student taken the time to go online and visit the Environmental Protection Agency's Web page before talking with the official, he would have learned that the EPA definitely considers asbestos something to be concerned about. In fact he would have learned that there are 500,000 asbestos cases currently in the nation's court system, with another 250 being filed daily. So when the official told the student reporter the university was really more concerned with painting than removing asbestos, the student could have asked him something like this: "Really, but with 500,000 asbestos cases currently in the courts and another 250 being filed daily, *shouldn't* the university be concerned about that asbestos?" It's doubtful the official would have had a coherent comeback, because he would have been caught flat-footed, as he deserved to be, for taking the low road when it came to this very serious issue. All the man had to do was assure the student reporter that the university was following federal guidelines (which it was) in the removal of the asbestos, and for that reason the university felt any safety concern was being properly addressed.

USING THE REAL PERSON'S INTERVIEW TO HELP DIRECT THE COURSE OF THE STORY

Had the student reporting on the asbestos story done his interviewing homework, he also could have used his real person to good advantage regarding the issues with which many in his audience would have been concerned. That's the function of the real person—to bring us into the story on a personal level. As it was, this is how the student reporter set up his real person: TIM HUMLIN WORKS IN FARLEY HALL. HE SAYS THE CONSTRUCTION IS AN INCONVENIENCE. Yes, lung cancer could be an "inconvenience," but of course, there was nothing to be concerned about. After all, the "main project over there" was really only repainting the windows. The sound bite chosen from the real person's interview was one that had the effect of diminishing a serious story even more: "With all the warm weather, it's really hot in here, and you can't open the windows."

Had the reporting student done his homework, he could have used the information obtained from the Internet to ask more serious, more logical questions of his real person: Do you know asbestos is considered a cancer-causing material by the EPA? You didn't? How does that make you feel about the work going on here? Did you know it's a material that's easily airborne? You didn't? Do you think that yellow tape would have much impact in that case? Those questions would definitely have elicited responses that addressed the issues of concern to any thinking person working in and around the building where the asbestos was being removed. And no, they're not leading, but logical, because these are the concerns of the EPA regarding public safety.

Armed with the logical questions for his interview and having elicited logical responses, the reporter would have been able to set his real person up something like this: TIM HUMLIN IS A CAMPUS RADIO D-J WHO WORKS A THREE-HOUR SHIFT EVERY DAY IN FARLEY HALL. HE HADN'T THOUGHT MUCH ABOUT ASBESTOS UNTIL NOW. HE SAYS HE'S A BIT CONCERNED. His actuality addressing the yellow-tape question might then go something like this: "I don't know much about it, but if that stuff's in the air, I don't see how that yellow tape is going to help." The student reporter might then have asked the university official about how much protection that yellow tape could be expected to provide. The issue would have been given a proper foundation because of the concern expressed by the real person. Use your real person by asking those questions you know the real people of your audience would ask if they were in your place.

Use your real person questions to bring up the issues you want to cover in your story. Remember, you're not an essayist or an editorialist. You gather the logical information necessary to tell the story. One of the people you gather that information from is your real person. Finally, avoid letting your real person *preach* to the audience. By that, I mean if your real person is doing something like donating blood, your audience doesn't want to be told by the real person that they, too, should give blood. Your audience wants to know *why* that person gives. Your audience is more likely to respond positively to a personal experience than to an admonition.

INTERVIEW THE RIGHT REAL PERSON

Reporting students will often blame their interviewing problems on dull or uncooperative interviewees. "I couldn't get anything out of him," or "That's what he said. I can't tell him what to say," is a common excuse. Since the real person is brought into the story by the reporter, and asked to be a part of the story by the reporter, it's obviously the reporter's responsibility to locate a real person who can address the issue at hand from a personal perspective. You, the reporter, pick the people you interview. Take the time to locate the best possible real person for your story; then ask those questions that will get real answers.

INTERVIEWING TIPS

1. Ask one clear and concise question at a time.
2. Listen to your interviewee.
3. Develop a sense of curiosity if you don't have one, because without it, you'll never be a very good interviewer and, consequently, never be a very good writer. That's why curiosity tops the list. Curiosity. Never fail to wonder "why?" As Metzler says, "A creative interviewer, guided by lively curiosity, never runs out of questions."
4. It's okay to ask questions that can be answered with a "yes" or a "no," but be sure to follow up with "why?"
5. Always look your interviewee in the eye. However, people don't like to be stared at; that's another good reason to have your reporter's pad of questions available. It's natural to look at it and occasionally jot down notes. But never look away to the left or right; that indicates boredom.
6. Ask your questions in a conversational manner. One student prefaced each question in his interview with the phrase "question one, question two," and so on. Don't do that.

7. Do not read your questions from your notebook, but paraphrase them, and again, ask them conversationally.

8. Avoid antagonizing your interviewee by blunt questioning. A good way to avoid the personal confrontation when questioning officials is to use the phrase "What do you say to those who say . . ."

9. Don't take the spontaneity out of your recorded interview by asking the questions you plan to ask before the tape is rolling. This means you should develop the ability to engage in small talk, asking the interviewee questions that are not a part of the story. Commenting about artwork or trophies or family photos that are often featured in a person's office also makes a good conversational gambit until you're ready to roll tape.

10. Dress appropriately. Ill-chosen attire can speak volumes—before you open your mouth to ask your first question.

11. Don't blame your interviewee. If you're not getting the kind of answers you'd like, most likely you aren't asking the kind of questions it takes to get those answers.

12. After your interview, ask yourself what was the most intriguing thing your interviewee said. Trust your instincts. If it intrigues you, trust that it will intrigue your audience as well.

SUMMARY

The interview can make or break your story. Develop a sense of curiosity about those you interview, especially the real persons. Ask personal questions of your real persons. They aren't expert about anything except their *own* experience. Use real persons to introduce questions that allow *you* to explore the issues of the story (e.g., the asbestos story). Ask questions of the official that will give you the *overview* of the story. In most cases, your questions to the official will be *impersonal*. Always write a list of questions before doing any interview so that you'll know what part each interviewee plays in your story, what your story is about, and how you can use the interviewees to tell your story.

CHAPTER QUIZ 1

Demonstrate your understanding of the real person concept of interviewing.

1. Whom should you interview first—the real person or the official?

2. To whom would you pose the following question: How has your life changed since the casinos came to town?
   a. real person
   b. official

3. To whom would you pose the following question: What problems has the power outage caused the city?
   a. real person
   b. official

4. In a story about a block grant to improve the neighborhood, which question listed below would you be least likely to ask your real person?
   a. What would you expect this grant to achieve in your neighborhood?
   b. How long have you lived here?
   c. Do you have any children?

5. In a story about rapes being committed in a certain area of your city, which question would you be least likely to ask the real person?
   a. Are the police doing all they can do?
   b. Are the women in your family taking any special precautions?
   c. What do you think makes a person commit such a crime?

6. In a story about voter apathy, which question would you be least likely to ask your real person?
   a. Do you plan to vote? Why? Why not?
   b. What issues are you interested in that you think the candidates aren't addressing?
   c. Why do you think only a small percentage of voters are expected to participate?

7. In a story about residents protesting a topless bar in their neighborhood, which question would you be least likely to ask your real person?
   a. Why do you think men attend such bars?
   b. What harm does it do your children, given the fact that it's located here?
   c. Do you think it affects the value of your house?

8. In a story about rising gasoline prices, which question would you be least likely to ask your real person?
   a. Will this affect your vacation travel?
   b. How many miles a year do you normally put on your car?
   c. Should Congress penalize the oil producing nations for the continued increase in the price of crude oil?

9. True or false: In a story about capital punishment, all the questions listed below would be acceptable to ask of your real person.
   a. Could you pull the switch or lethally inject the convicted person?
   b. How do you feel about capital punishment?
   c. What can society do to correct the mistake if an innocent person is executed?

10. In a story about prayer in public schools, which question would you be least likely to ask your real person?
    a. How do you feel about prayer in public schools?
    b. What do you think people who are opposed to it should do?
    c. What problems do you see in a constitutional amendment that would make prayer a constitutional right in public schools?

CHAPTER QUIZ 2

Keeping in mind that you want your real person to respond from a personal point of view—that is, his or her personal experience of the larger story you are reporting—circle the most appropriate question to ask of a real person.

1. College students are being interviewed about the school's new library.
   a. How do you think most students will react to the library improvements?
   b. What's your favorite improvement to the library?

2. Teenagers are being interviewed about teenage drinking.
   a. Why do you think teenagers drink?
   b. Did you ever have an experience where you were in a car with a friend who was driving drunk? What happened?

3. Neighborhood watch participants are being interviewed about the program.
   a. Was there anything that convinced you to get involved with your neighborhood watch?
   b. What do you think the function of a neighborhood watch program should be?

4. Women are being interviewed about anorexia.
   a. Why do you think women become anorexic?
   b. Could you see yourself becoming anorexic?

5. People are being interviewed about gun control.
   a. Do you keep a gun in your house? Why? Why not?
   b. What kind of legislation do you think the government should pass?

6. People are being interviewed about abortion legislation.
   a. What do you think would happen if the legislation were repealed?
   b. Are there any circumstances under which you could see yourself getting an abortion? Why? Why not?

7. Bank personnel are being interviewed following a robbery.
   a. How did you feel when you saw him waving that shotgun around?
   b. What did they do when they came in?

8. Homeowners are being interviewed about raising taxes to fund schools.

   a. So where do you think the taxes should come from?

   b. You don't have kids? How do you feel about having to fund the school system?

9. People are being interviewed about capital punishment.

   a. Do you think society as a whole benefits from capital punishment?

   b. What if it were your wife or your child?

10. People are being interviewed about an upcoming art and music festival.

   a. What's your favorite part of the festival?

   b. Why do you think the festival always draws so many people to town?

CHAPTER 9

Putting It All Together in the TV Script

PUTTING PICTURES TO YOUR WORDS

Every sentence of your TV report has to be written in the context of how you will visually illustrate that sentence. In short, you must now think visually.

PEOPLE-IZED PICTURES

So where do these pictures come from? Think people. Think real persons and it should become obvious to you that a major source for pictures is your real person. The fact that your story needs pictures makes it even more obvious that you should introduce your real person into your narrative as soon as possible, just as you did in your radio reports. The sooner you get to your real person, the sooner you will have pictures to illustrate the story that will make your story human.

Let's return to Wilma Jones in Tunica. Instead of just hearing her, now we will see her. Doing what? Hosting at Splash Casino. Two things to remember: We don't want to fall into the predictable pattern of beginning with our real person, and we always want to open with the most logical and visually interesting video. So we could use the same natural-sound opening that was used in our radio report, but this time we will supply the pictures as well. Natural sound provides the ambience (atmosphere) we need to give our stories presence. So we open with close-ups of a roulette wheel spinning, slot machine windows lining up, and Wilma Jones walking by with a tray of drinks in her job as a casino hostess as our narrative begins: THAT'S THE SOUND OF MONEY IN TUNICA, MISSISSIPPI, THESE DAYS, AND IT'S MUSIC TO WILMA JONES'S EARS. A majority of the video could consist of sequences of Wilma walking from customer to customer serving drinks. We could also shoot a sequence of Wilma getting into her car and driving over recently paved roads or around road construction as we talk about the increased fees for city projects such as road improvements. And we could wrap up by showing Wilma shopping, which would be a fitting ending to our economic report on gambling in Tunica, Mississippi.

PUTTING YOUR REAL PERSON IN VISUAL ACTION

Do you just happen to grab Wilma in the act of doing her job? No. After getting permission from the casino management to shoot your video of Wilma at work, you arrange to meet her at a time when she'll be able to work with you. As with every real person used in your stories, Wilma will expect you to tell her what to do and when to do it. Some of your footage will no doubt capture Wilma doing her job without direction from you, except for the instruction to just do what she would normally do. But there will also be setup shots that will require you to ask Wilma to repeat an action so that you can get the shot from a different perspective (close-up, medium, cover) in order to facilitate continuity editing, that is, editing of action so that it looks natural.

USING THE LOGICAL ILLUSTRATIVE B-ROLL

The video we see of your real person must logically illustrate the narrative of your story. Your real person must be seen in a context that complements, rather than distracts from, the reporter's narrative.

A Case History

A student was covering a different angle of the aforementioned *Playboy* story. His story dealt with the fact that the sororities on campus were prohibiting their members from applying to pose for the men's magazine. His real person was a sorority member. The video showed her playing piano to the accompanying narrative: ONE SORORITY GIRL SAYS POSING FOR IT CONFLICTS WITH THE IDEALS OF THE SORORITY. LAURA LANGSTON SAYS IT GOES AGAINST A LOT OF WHAT HER SORORITY WAS FOUNDED ON.

What does playing piano have to do with the story the reporter is telling? Is what the audience is seeing typical of how we think of sorority members and their activities at college? In other words, is the illustrative b-roll of this story logical? No. What might we have seen that would be more representative of sorority members and college? How about playing Frisbee with fellow students in front of the student union? How about hanging out with fellow students in the union? How about going to class, being in class, simply walking across campus? The student defended his choice of illustrative video by saying he just wanted to do something more creative than the expected. That's fine. But, again, the video has to make sense to his audience.

How might he have used this piano video logically? Again, every picture we use to illustrate our story must have a logical connection to the story, must support our narrative. Let's think about *Playboy*. What kind of copy usually accompanies *Playboy* layouts? One that readily comes to mind is the "turn-ons/turnoffs" of the foldout. With that in mind, our student reporter might have written something like this: PLAYBOY IS HOLDING AUDITIONS THIS WEEKEND FOR ITS WOMEN OF THE S-E-C CALENDAR. SOPHOMORE LAURA LANGSTON IS A MEMBER OF A SORORITY. TURN-ONS—PLAYING PIANO, ESPECIALLY FOR HER SORORITY SISTERS. TURNOFFS—THE THOUGHT OF HUGH HEFNER WITH MANDY AND CANDY—AND THE FACT THAT HE HOPES TO GET OLE MISS FEMALES TO TAKE OFF THEIR CLOTHES FOR HIS MAGAZINE. Now the piano playing makes sense, but only because of the accompanying narrative. In order for your TV story to work, the audio must complement the video and vice versa.

This particular story also featured several shots of a formal living room setting devoid of people. Many students found that confusing when they viewed the story in class. Why was the reporter showing them this "furniture"? The reporter explained the shots were of the interior of the sorority house to which his real person belonged. He said the sorority house was not named because his real person did not want to associate her sorority with *Playboy*, nor did her sisters want to be seen in the story. That information should have been shared with his audience in his narrative. It would have made the shots of the furniture logical, though still rather static. The lesson here: stay with the *people* of your story.

STAY WITH THE PEOPLE

Avoid static shots of *things* in illustrating your story. Again, if you remember that people are interested in people, you will keep them in your video and you will keep your video interesting as well as human. For instance, if you're covering Mardi Gras, don't show your audience an isolated shot of a sign advertising nude dancing; instead, show the great number of people walking by that sign as they hustle through the French Quarter. Your audience will see the sign, but your story won't have stopped.

If you're covering a story on a painting exhibit at a gallery, don't simply take shots of the paintings. Incorporate the people viewing the paintings and create sequences of a person walking past other paintings to look at a particular painting. Your framed TV shot of the painting will never do the painting justice. It will not substitute for seeing the painting in person, so make your video the vehicle for showing the scale of the paintings, the interest in the paintings, the location, and so on. If you're covering Election Day activities, don't show an isolated sign of an arrow pointing to where the poll is located; show people walking to the poll. A good rule of thumb is to avoid signs in general. People-ize your videos.

THE STAND-UP

The stand-up is your time in the spotlight. The stand-up is that part of the TV package where you, the reporter, face the camera and speak directly to your audience. It is the place where you take credit for your story. It puts you on the scene as the fact gatherer. The information contained in your stand-up should advance the story by contributing additional, pertinent information.

The Transition Stand-up

The most effective stand-up is one that comes near the middle of your story. It generally serves as a transition from one sound bite to the next. The best options for the stand-up are after the first real person sound bite and before the official, or after the official and before the second real person sound bite.

Stand-up Content

The transitional stand-up can be tricky, since you're usually writing it before you've written the beginning of your story. However, while it may not follow the logical rules of writing as you have known them, the information in your stand-up should continue the narrative of the story in a logical fashion. The biggest advantage of a transitional stand-up is that it forces you, the reporter, to think about the structure of your story *while* you are still on the scene of the story. You must ask yourself, How do I plan to begin this story? How will I end it? Where will my stand-up information come from? Most likely, it will come from the interviews you did with either your official or your real person. That's why it's always good to have a handheld tape recorder with you when doing interviews. While still on the scene, you can listen to what these people said, then paraphrase them in your stand-up. Or your stand-up content could come from your research—say, information from the Internet. Wherever it comes from, remember to write it down. Not to read on camera, but to aid you in memorizing your stand-up. This way you're sure to include all the information you intended to include.

Making the Stand-up Visual

Make sure your stand-up includes a visually logical background. For example, in our Tunica story, part of the information we've gathered tells us the roads into and out of Tunica have been damaged by increased traffic. So traffic on the road behind you would make a logical background as you tell your audience about the increased fees to maintain the roads. The new shopping mall would also make a logical background as you relay that aspect of the story.

Another background might be simply symbolic. For instance, if your story has to do with university plans for new scholarships, your stand-up might be in front of the university's administrative offices, since this is where such decisions are made.

Use a prop when you can. For example, you might refer to a scholarship application that you hold in your hand as you tell your audience what it takes to qualify for one of these new scholarships.

Move when you can. You don't appear as stiff when you are walking and talking as you might when you're simply standing and talking to the camera. Your walking should incorporate an aspect of the story. For example, if you're talking about litter on a public lakeshore, you might scoop up a piece of trash and throw it into a garbage container as you tell your audience: Park rangers say an average of ten tons of garbage litters the lakeshore every summer.

Finally, because you want to have as much presence as possible when on camera, be sure that the camera frames you prominently in the foreground, preferably from the waist up with proper headroom.

THE TV SCRIPT

Unlike the radio script, the TV script is written in separate columns designating audio and video portions of the script. Each station will have some variation of the two-column format. However, because of the advent of teleprompters, the format's all-caps standard has been losing favor over the years. In an informal e-mail survey, we found a number of stations have dropped the all-caps typing, though many still retain it because their anchors prefer it and because it is also a standard of closed-captioned TV. We use the all-caps approach in this book because it is still commonly practiced and because it helps make clear when we are designating script that's meant to be read by an anchor or reporter.

The TV reporter will cover and turn in up to three stories a day, especially in the smaller markets where staffs are usually at a minimum and so expected to do more. Those three stories can require three different formats: (1) the *package* format (see box 9.1), (2) the *VO/SOT* format (see box 9.2), and (3) the *VO* format. The package will incorporate all the elements we've talked about in this chapter (i.e., anchor lead, reporter narrative, real person, and official sound bites and stand-up). It will normally be no more than *two* double-columned pages only. The VO/SOT is a story condensed to its essence. There will be no real person narrative, and the sound bite will usually feature the official. It will average about thirty seconds and will consist of about four sentences, one SOT, and a one- or two-sentence wrap-up. Though the reporter writes the VO/SOT script, the anchor reads it live in its entirety, except, of course, for the sound bite. It normally consists of *one* page only. Your audience will usually have no idea you had anything to do with the report since they will neither hear your voice nor see your face. The anchor will also read the *VO* (*voice over the video*), which will average twenty seconds or less and will not include a sound bite.

BOX 9.1 *Sample TV News Script–Package*

REPORTER: Jane Doe
VIDEOGRAPHER: Jack Smith
SLUG: Tunica Gambling Economy

VIDEO	AUDIO
ANCHOR ON CAMERA *TAKE ENG	ANC: CITIZENS OF TUNICA COUNTY HAVE BEEN RIDING THE WHEEL OF FORTUNE FOR OVER A YEAR NOW—EVER SINCE LEGALIZED GAMBLING CAME TO TOWN. AS JANE DOE REPORTS, IT'S HAD A POSITIVE ECONOMIC EFFECT ON WHAT WAS ONCE THE POOREST COUNTY IN THE NATION.*
CLOSE UP OF ROULETTE WHEEL AND SLOTS	N/S (gambling noises)
WILMA SERVING DRINKS	V: THINGS ARE JUMPING IN TUNICA THESE DAYS. AND WILMA JONES COULDN'T BE HAPPIER. THE MOTHER OF THREE HAD BEEN OUT OF WORK FOR THREE YEARS. SHE WAS BEGINNING TO DOUBT SHE'D EVER WORK AGAIN. THAT WAS BEFORE SPLASH CAME TO TOWN.
Wilma Jones Casino Hostess	SOT: I was on food stamps. It was tough.
WILMA SHOPPING WITH CHILDREN	V: WILMA JONES IS ONE OF 15-HUNDRED TUNICA RESIDENTS WHO LEFT THE UNEMPLOYMENT ROLL TO BECOME PART OF SPLASH CASINO'S PAYROLL. ALONG WITH THE NEW JOBS HAS COME A NEW CONSUMERISM.
Jim Smith Mall Manager	SOT: We would never have built here if not for the casinos.
Jane Doe, Stand-up	SOT: But Tunica's new prosperity does have its downside. A major issue is the increase in traffic as people flock from all over to Tunica's gambling tables. Taxes have been increased to upgrade and maintain the county's road system.
WILMA GETTING INTO CAR	V: WILMA JONES SAYS THAT DOESN'T BOTHER HER.
Wilma Jones	SOT: At least now I got a paycheck to take the taxes out of.
WILMA DRIVING A NEW CAR PAST ROAD CONSTRUCTION	V: SHE ALSO HAS A NEW CAR TO DRIVE OVER—AND AROUND—NEW ROAD CONSTRUCTION. IT'S BEEN JUST OVER A YEAR SINCE GAMBLING CAME TO TOWN, AND CITIZENS LIKE WILMA JONES ARE BETTING ON TUNICA'S CONTINUED PROSPERITY. JANE DOE, W-X-X-X NEWS.

BOX 9.2 *Sample TV News Script–VO/SOT*

REPORTER: Jane Doe
SLUG: Tunica Gambling Economy

VIDEO	AUDIO
ANCHOR ON CAMERA *TAKE VIDEO SHOPPERS AT MALL	GAMBLERS HAVE BEEN BETTING ON TUNICA, MISSISSIPPI, FOR JUST OVER A YEAR NOW.* OFFICIALS SAY LEGALIZED GAMBLING HAS HAD A POSITIVE ECONOMIC AFFECT ON THE COUNTY. FOR THE FIRST TIME IN A LONG TIME, MANY RESIDENTS ARE EMPLOYED. ABOUT 15-HUNDRED ARE EMPLOYED BY THE CASINOS. ABOUT 400 WORK AT THE NEW MALL.
Jim Smith Manager Tunica Mall	SOT: We would never have built there if not for the casinos. People have money to spend, we have what they want, so it works out well all around.
SHOTS OF SANITATION TRUCK	VO: RESIDENTS ARE PAYING HIGHER FEES FOR CITY SERVICES BECAUSE OF THE INCREASED ACTIVITY. HOWEVER, OFFICIALS SAY THEY'VE HAD FEW COMPLAINTS.

SUMMARY

Use your real person to illustrate as much of your story as possible. Put the real person in action as soon as possible to make sure you grab your audience's attention as soon as possible. Using your real person to illustrate your story helps you avoid shooting boring shots of static things like buildings and signs. Don't be afraid to direct your real person on camera to get the shots you'll need to illustrate the story.

Often a TV reporter will write a story, then have to go out on another one and not be available to tell the editor how the story is supposed to go together. The editor who gets the story will know how it's supposed to be edited by the format of the script. The TV script is written in two columns to facilitate the collaborative process. The scripts in this book are written in all caps, which is the traditional method. The larger type facilitates the anchor's reading. While many stations retain the traditional method, others are beginning to phase it out, citing improved teleprompters and the need to cut and paste printed text into their online Web pages.

CHAPTER QUIZ 1

1. The biggest difference between writing a report for radio and writing one for TV is that the TV reporter must think _____ .

2. When it comes to illustrating your story, which source affords the best visual opportunity, the real person or the official?

3. True or false: You should never direct your real person in order to get the shots you need to illustrate the story.

4. True or false: You should always start your reporter narrative by referencing your real person in the first sentence.

5. True or false: It's a good idea to shoot static shots of things rather than people.

6. Natural sound provides the _____ that gives your story presence.

7. A TV script is written in _____ columns.

8. The left column of the TV script lists the _____ of your story.

9. The right column of the TV script lists the _____ of your story.

10. The sooner you introduce your real person visually into your story, the sooner you make your story _____ .

11. The reporter should be framed from _____ and featured prominently in the foreground.

12. The VO/SOT is narrated by the _____ .

13. The VO/SOT's average length is about _____ .

14. True or false: A VO/SOT does not include a real person narrative.

15. The _____ reads the VO/SOT live.

16. A VO/SOT is _____ page(s) only.

17. How many pages will a package normally consist of?

18. The _____ reads the VO.

19. A VO is normally _____ seconds or less.

20. True or false: The VO/SOT format is just a shortened version of a package format.

CHAPTER QUIZ 2

1. Using the story information from chapter 12, exercise 1 (property reappraisal), write a script using the TV package format. See the model in box 9.1 (p. 79).

2. Using the story information from chapter 12, exercise 1 (property reappraisal), write a script using the TV VO/SOT format. See the model in box 9.2 (p. 80).

CHAPTER 10

Critical Evaluation

EXAMINING THE ELEMENTS

As we have learned, there are specific elements that go into writing a news story and particularly a *humanized* news story. You must be constantly aware of them as you write. A broadcast journalist doesn't really have the luxury of writing a *first draft* from beginning to end. This means you must learn to revise on the fly. If you pay attention to the elements and commit them to practice, you'll not only tell better stories; you'll write them faster.

But you're not a broadcast journalist yet. As a student, you're usually meeting weekly deadlines instead of daily deadlines. So you have the time to take your reports apart and put them back together. Now is the time to get *critical*.

Sentences

You've written your story and you're ready to edit that radio or TV report. Don't. Not until you take a good long look at each of the sentences you've written. You've probably written a total of ten sentences for that radio report, maybe twelve for that TV story. Make sure each sentence follows the preceding sentence *logically*.

Look at each sentence. Count the number of words in each. Are there more than twenty words in any of them? If there are, take the time to rewrite those sentences. Words can usually be dropped from sentences that are not constructed in the order of subject, verb, object. Tightly structure subject-verb-object sentences. Check for commas. If you've written a sentence with one or more commas, chances are you've made it more complex than it should be. It's also likely your sentence includes more than *just one thought*. Remember, your sentences should contain *one* thought only. Use contractions. Contractions not only transform two words into one, but also make you sound more *conversational*. Follow broadcast style.

Sound Bites or Actualities

Take a look at your sound bites as transcribed in your script. Do they contain *one* thought only? They should. Check them for redundancy. Is the interviewee repeating what you wrote in your lead-in to the sound bite or actuality?

A Case History

A student wrote, STUDENT TORRY THOMAS SAYS SHE'S WORRIED ABOUT WHAT JOBS WILL BE AVAILABLE WHEN SHE GRADUATES and then transitioned to Torry saying "I am *worried* that, you know, I'm a marketing major, and when things don't sell, we're the first ones to get cut." Notice how the word "worried" stands out as an echo when heard again in the sound bite. Much better to begin the sound bite one thought later, where the student says: "I'm a marketing major."

Later in this same story about career day and getting a job after graduation, the student wrote, in reference to career day, SHE SAYS IT WILL HELP EASE SOME OF THE PRESSURES OF JOB HUNTING, and then transitioned to his second real person sound bite, in which Torry said, "I'm really *worried* that the jobs won't be out there for me, but I really am glad that I'm able to get out there and see what's out there beforehand, though." That's the third "worried" in the student's story. Again, a little judicious editing, along with remembering to use only *one* thought per sound bite, would have resulted in eliminating that second redundancy by starting the sound bite one thought later: "I really am glad that I'm able . . ."

CRITICAL EVALUATION CHECKLIST

Sentences and sound bites or actualities are the major building blocks of your story. The information those sentences and sound bites contain and the order in which they are presented will determine if your story structure will stand or fall. Box 10.1 includes a critical evaluation checklist to guide you throughout the writing and structuring of your story.

BOX 10. 1   *Critical Evaluation Checklist*

1. **Do any sentences contain more than twenty words?**
   Count the words in each of the sentences you write, remembering that you are going to have to read them. The more words you write, the more potential stumbling blocks in your path, and the more breath you're going to need to get through the sentence.
   Y_____   N_____

2. **Do any sentences contain more than one thought?**
   When you try to put more than one thought into a sentence, you risk making the sentence more complex than it should be. You risk making it difficult for you to read, and you risk making it difficult for your listener to follow.
   Y_____   N_____

3. **Do sentences follow the subject–verb–object order?**
   The tighter your sentence structure, the less room for confusion.
   Y_____   N_____

4. **Is the anchor lead sentence present tense?**
   Broadcast news is immediate. Present tense gives broadcast news the *sound* of immediacy.
   Y_____   N_____

5. **Is there an actor in action in the anchor lead's opening sentence?**
   Taking the time to decide who the actor is in your anchor lead gives you the first words you'll put down on that blank screen. Knowing what the action is gives you an immediate destination, so you write that crucial first sentence much faster. And because of its subject-verb-object construction, your sentence will be much more succinct and will generally require fewer words.
   Y_____   N_____

6. **Does the first sentence of the anchor lead give you a good indication of what the story to come is about?**
   Your anchor lead is a contract with your audience. In it, you tell your audience what the story to come is about. That first anchor sentence should contain the overriding fact of your story. It should logically set up the second anchor lead sentence.
   Y_____   N_____

7. **Does the second anchor sentence more narrowly focus the story to come?**
   The second anchor sentence must logically build on the first. Together, they should make clear what the story to come is all about.
   Y_____   N_____

8. **Does the reporter's first sentence logically follow the anchor lead setup?**
   The first sentence of the reporter narrative must follow the direction set up by the second anchor sentence. One sentence should flow logically into the other without redundancy.
   Y_____   N_____

9. **Is the information logically organized?**
   Give us the information we need when we need it. Give us all of the logical information required of your story. Don't raise questions that you don't immediately answer. Don't digress to issues that aren't directly related to the story you're telling.
   Y_____   N_____

—continued on page 86

Critical Evaluation Checklist continued from page 85

10. Does the writer transition to the real person at the earliest possible moment (preferably by the reporter's second sentence)?

The sooner you transition to your real person, the sooner you put a "face" on your story and make it more than just a collection of facts. Make every effort to bring your real person in by the second sentence of your reporter narration.

Y_____ N_____

11. Are the sentences setting up the real person personal?

The two sentences setting up your real person should refer directly to the real person. In those sentences your audience should learn something personal about the real person that relates to the issue you are covering in the larger story. For example, if you're talking about a property tax increase, then you would tell your audience how much property tax your real person is currently paying and how much he or she will pay after the increase. Then your real person's actuality or sound bite would continue that thought.

Y_____ N_____

12. Does the real person's actuality or sound bite contain more than one thought?

Any more than one thought in an actuality or sound bite and your interviewee can begin to sound rambling; your story can take an arbitrary turn. *You* must control the selection and placement of the words of your interviewee just as *you* control the placement and the selection of the words in your sentences.

Y_____ N_____

13. Does the real person's actuality or sound bite support the anchor lead's premise?

Unless your real person's sound bite refers directly back *to* your anchor lead, you are not telling us the story you promised in your anchor lead. Whatever your real person says must reflect the theme your anchor lead sets up.

Y_____ N_____

14. Does the official's actuality or sound bite contain more than one thought?

Again, more than one thought in a sound bite or actuality, and your story may start to drag or take an unintended turn. Control the words of your sound bite as you control the words of your sentences.

Y_____ N_____

15. Does the official's actuality or sound bite support the anchor lead's premise?

Just as your real person's sound bite must support the premise established in your anchor lead, so must the official sound bite. It has to refer directly to the anchor lead or your structure has cracked.

Y_____ N_____

16. Does the story include all necessary attribution?

Your job is to report, not generalize. As a general rule, don't tell your audience anything you can't attribute to a source—either the real person or official of your story or some other documentation. We're not interested in your opinions or your generalizations. We're only interested in you as a reporter, in your ability to explore issues and present the facts cohesively and humanly.

Y_____ N_____

17. Do the facts of the story support the anchor lead?

The *people* in your audience want you to tell a human story, and they want you to do it with facts. They expect your story to contain all the factual information germane to the story you promised them in your anchor lead.

Y_____ N_____

18. Are there style errors?

Style counts. It helps you write and read succinctly.

Y_____ N_____

Check your work against this checklist for every story you write.

SUMMARY

Certain elements are common to all news stories. Become familiar with these elements. They'll help you create a soundly structured story. They'll help make your story human. Be critical of your own writing. Eventually, you'll develop your own checklist, a subconscious one that will keep your story on course.

CHAPTER 11

Shooting and Editing TV News Video

AN ART AND A CRAFT

In the very bad movie *"Manos" the Hands of Fate*, featured in the *Mystery Science 3000* series, a man drives a car down a lonely country road, and he drives, and he drives, and he drives, and he drives. One can only figure that the director wanted to get the idea across that it was a long, long way to this particular destination. The director knew *what* he wanted to shoot; he just didn't know *how* to shoot it, affording the little characters down front in *Mystery Science's* theater some very funny ad-libs. Now that you know *what* to shoot, you need to know *how* to shoot, and then edit what you've shot so that your production avoids the fate of *Manos*.

You should know from the outset that the process of shooting and editing is not only a craft, but an art as well. Some rare students can pick a camera up for the first time and, once instructed in its use, can almost immediately begin shooting not only acceptable footage, but exceptional footage. Equally, there are those who take to editing because they find it a creative outlet, while others find it tedious. But because shooting and editing are also crafts, there are certain rules that, if followed, can help make you both an acceptable shooter and editor.

CAPTURING THE SHOT

The most fundamental element of video-taping is the shot. A shot is that amount of video that is captured between the time you push the button to start your camera and the time you push the button to stop it. A rule of thumb is that an isolated shot should last no longer than three to five seconds. When these shots are part of a *sequence* (which we will get to), they may be longer or shorter. However, you should roll tape for at least twenty-five seconds on each shot, figuring that the part of the shot you

FIGURE 11.1   The head-and-shoulders shot.

will use will be the steady three to five seconds in the middle of that twenty-five-second shot. That's because the first ten seconds of your shot is apt to be shaky, as is the last ten seconds (the result of turning the camera on and turning it off).

FRAMING THE SHOT

You, as the shooter, determine how much is visible in the shot or frame at any given moment. Effective framing eliminates distractions while engaging the viewer. This is particularly true of one of the most standard shots in TV news—the interview shot.

The Interview Shot

This shot is also known as the *head-and-shoulders* or *talking head* shot, because, as the person talks, the only parts of the person visible in the frame are her head and shoulders. The inter-viewee is framed slightly off center with at least three-quarters of her face showing as she faces the off-camera reporter. This means that your camera must be placed slightly behind the reporter (preferably on a tripod) and as near to his (left or right) shoulder as possible without including him in the shot. There must be enough *lead space* in the direction that the interviewee is looking to make the shot psychologically comfortable. The viewer begins to feel hemmed in if the interviewee's nose is too close to the edge of the frame as she looks in the direction of the off-camera reporter. Additionally, the interviewee must have the appro-priate *headroom*, that space between the top of the person's head and the top of the TV frame. Too much headroom will make the person look insignificant. Not enough, and the person's head will look as though it is being confined and even pressed down upon by the top of the TV frame (see figure 11.1).

The Over-the-Shoulder Shot

This shot should be framed from the same camera location as your interview shot and should be taped before

FIGURE 11.2   The over-the-shoulder shot.

the actual interview begins, while the reporter is engaged in small talk with the interviewee. Once you have the interviewee framed for the interview, simply zoom back until the back of the reporter's head and his left or right shoulder are visible in the foreground with the interviewee looking toward the reporter (see figure 11.2). Once you have at least thirty seconds of this shot, stop your camera and zoom back into the interview framing and advise the reporter you are ready to begin taping the interview. The shot is used as a bridge that allows the reporter to give an additional three to five seconds of voiceover setup information before the shot cuts to the talking head (see figure 11.2).

The Stand-up Shot

In the previous chapter, we talked about the importance of the stand-up in telling your story. This is your opportunity to visually take credit for your story, so you should always be framed with presence, even if you're doing a walking stand-up. Always make sure that by the time you are delivering the last few words, you have walked close enough to the camera to be prominently framed either screen left or screen right when you stop and finish what you have to say. You want to be sure you are framed from about the waist up with proper headroom. Similarly, if the building you're using as your background is important to the story (and it should be if you're using it), include its whole façade and give yourself presence at the same time by moving both your camera and yourself far enough away from

the building to frame you prominently in the foreground with much
of the building's façade visible behind you either screen left or screen
right (see figure 11.3).

The B-roll Shots

These are the individual shots
that serve to illustrate your overall story. When shooting b-roll,
remember that the people featured in it must have proper lead
space and headroom, just as in
your interview shots. For instance,
if you're shooting a person walk-

FIGURE 11.3 The stand-up shot.

ing, be sure to allow space for her to walk into, so that it does not look as though she will
bump up against the side of the frame she's walking toward. And always strive to keep
people in your illustrative video rather than isolated shots of things like signs or buildings.
Again, *people* are interested in *people*.

SHOOTING TECHNIQUE

When shooting b-roll, always keep in mind that old adage that one picture is worth a
thousand words, because it is true. Your shots can be a thousand positive words that
support the story you're telling or a thousand negative words that detract from it. To make
sure all your pictures inspire those positive words, be sure to:

Use a Tripod

Shaky handheld shots are distracting. The shakiness is even more a problem if you stand
away from your subject and zoom in. That's why you should always use a tripod and move
in as close to the action as possible.

Limit Camera Movement

Remember your grandfather's home movies, with all that distracting zooming, panning, and
tilting? Zooming is using the camera's zoom lens to move in on a subject or out from it.

Panning refers to sweeping your camera lens across the scene horizontally; tilting is doing the same thing vertically. With all due respect to your gramps, all that movement is the sure sign of an amateur. Zoom, tilt, or pan only when you have a logical reason to do so.

Use Manual Focus

The problem with automatic focus is that it keeps trying to compensate for movement, and so goes in and out of focus, especially if there are moving objects in the foreground. Instead, set your focus by zooming in and focusing manually on details (eyebrows, lips); then zoom back to frame your shot.

Be Light Conscious

Use lights when you can, especially in an office interview situation. If the person you're interviewing has a window behind him, be sure to draw the blinds or else he will be dark, because your camera will expose for the window light and not the subject. Outside, avoid shooting subjects that have the sun *behind* them. Your subject will be silhouetted. Make sure the light source is behind *you*.

Be Audio Aware

Natural or ambient sound lends a live quality to every shot of your video as it stands alone or as the reporter narrates over. A shot without natural sound sounds unnatural. Most in-camera microphones do an acceptable job of picking up general sounds during taping, but if possible use a separate handheld or lapel mike to get good, clear audio when interviewing.

Get Close

Nothing draws us into the story better than a good close-up. Don't stand on the edge of your story: get personal, get close.

Shoot Enough

Remember, the average TV news report is about 1:15 to 1:30 in length (including the interviews). Each sentence you write will likely be three to five seconds long, so you'll need video to illustrate each of those sentences. If you consider that your average package will contain about twelve to sixteen sentences and multiply that by five, you can see that your story will require about a minute and twenty seconds' worth of video. Does that mean that's all the video you need to shoot for a story? Not by a long shot. As stated earlier, you need to make sure each shot you shoot lasts at least twenty-five seconds so that you will have the best part of the shot to choose from when you sit down to edit. Also, you will shoot the same shot from different angles and with different framing to give you editing options. There will also be those shots that just don't work and that you have to shoot again. One could easily shoot twenty minutes of b-roll to produce a seventy-five-second report.

Stay with the People

People keep your story visually interesting. Isolated shots of signs are boring and can distract viewers from the narrative as they try to read what a busy sign says. Shots of building façades can be very static. If you must shoot them, try to make sure people are walking by or entering the building.

Hit 'Em with Your Best Shot

Whenever possible, make the first shot of your report a grabber, a shot that will visually suck the audience into your report. For instance if you are covering Mardi Gras in New Orleans, a crowded street shot would be okay, but a street musician in the foreground with the crowd in the background would not only be more visually interesting, but would provide for good natural sound to open with as well. Then you could cut to medium and close-up shots of your crowd. When possible, do the same with your closing shot. Make it a shot that leaves a lasting impression.

Tell the People Story

Above all, remember you are telling a story about people. Be sensitive to the story elements that have the greatest impact, and try to capture them on video. For instance, a student was covering a story about the stress of taking the LSAT (Law School Admission Test). One of her best shots was of her real person just standing and looking out her window that somehow conveyed the feeling that her hopes and dreams were riding on the outcome.

SHOOTING FOR CONTINUITY

A single shot can be a scene, though a *series* of shots can also be a scene when shot for *continuity*. If movies weren't shot for continuity, you would find it hard to enjoy them. Continuity creates the *illusion* of uninterrupted action. Without continuity, actors would move erratically, *jump* from here to there, and generally violate every rule of time and space that has conditioned everyone's perception since birth. Yes, movies do sometimes violate this principle, but only when the director has a creative point to make.

FIGURE 11.4   The establishing shot.

In order to shoot for continuity, you must know the *three* basic shots—(1) establishing shot (also known as a cover or long shot), (2) medium shot, and (3) close-up shot. The framing of each of these shots can vary, but will always retain the characteristic of establishing, medium, or close-up. Additionally, you must know how to use the *cutaway* shot.

The Establishing Shot

Establishes the relationship of the people in the frame to their environment (see figure 11.4).

FIGURE 11.5   The medium shot.   FIGURE 11.6   The close-up shot.

The Medium Shot

Takes the audience closer to the action and eliminates visual distractions (see figure 11.5).

The Close-up Shot

Sometimes called a tight shot. It fills the screen and effectively captures a person's emotion or detail if your subject is inanimate (see figure 11.6).

The Cutaway Shot

This is usually a shot that is related to the main action but takes place in another location. For instance, the person playing with her cat on the porch notices a neighbor walking by (see figures 11.4–11.6) and the action cuts to that shot (see figure 11.7).

Screen Direction

There is an invisible line called the *axis line* or *vector line* that videographers need to keep in mind when shooting action. Crossing the line can result in disorienting your viewers by unexpectedly reversing screen direction. For instance, if a person is walking left to right in one shot, and then the video cuts to another shot where he is walking right to left, your viewer's expectation is disturbed, because your viewer suddenly sees the person walking toward himself. To avoid inadvertently changing screen direction while shooting, always keep the camera positioned on the side of the line from which you started shooting the action (see figure 11.8).

SHOOTING TO EDIT

Because TV news is such a deadline-driven medium, you need to think several steps ahead when writing or shooting. This means visualizing the story in your head before and during your shoot, so

FIGURE 11.7 The cutaway shot.

that you'll be able to edit much faster and with much better results. This is especially true when videotaping your real person. However, the same principle applies to the shooting of spot news—car crashes, fires—those spontaneous events happening in *real time*.

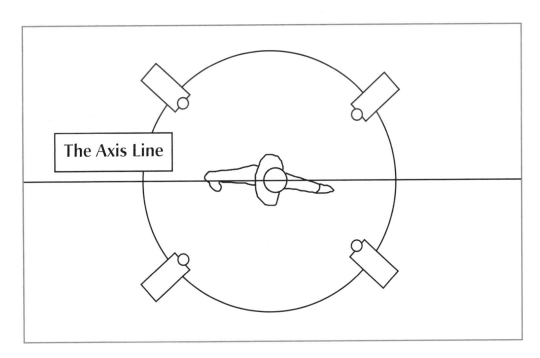

FIGURE 11.8 The axis line.

THINK LIKE A DIRECTOR

While you cannot, of course, direct real-time events, you can direct the real person of your story. In fact, once the real person agrees to cooperate with you, he or she will *expect* direction from you when it's time to shoot the b-roll. For example, Wilma Jones of the Tunica gambling story (see box 9.1) will expect you to tell her what to do—walk down that row of slot machines, serve that person a drink. In some instances you will have to direct the real person to do the same thing again, either because the action was awkward, or, more likely, because you have the establishing or long shot you want and now it's time to get a close-up shot (of the drink as the customer's hand reaches for it), or another close-up shot (as Wilma smiles at the customer) from the same or different angles. Why? Because our three *basic* shots lend variety to our video as they facilitate editing.

SHOOT SEQUENCES

Sequences eliminate jump cuts and compress real time. For example, if you have a cover shot of Wilma walking toward your camera, past it, and out of frame, you can then cut to a close-up shot of the tray of drinks Wilma is carrying as a hand comes into the frame to get the drink, then to the close-up of Wilma smiling at the customer, and finally to a cover shot of Wilma walking out of the shot as the customer who sits on his stool swings back to his slot machine. You can see a lot of wasted time and motion is eliminated in that sequence.

A sequence consists of two shots or more. For instance a shot of a person bending over a desk and filling out a form would be a sequence if you cut from the cover or medium shot of the person signing the form to a close-up of the person's hand as she continues to fill out the form. If you wanted to add a third shot, you could take a close-up profile shot of the person's face as she looks down at the form (which is not in the frame).

EDITING THE VIDEO

The straight cut is the most common edit in a TV news report, with a quick dissolve into each interview as well as into the stand-up. That means you simply cut from one shot to the next while editing the b-roll, with no fades, dissolves, or other special effects until you dissolve to the SOT.

THE EDIT DECISION

Do not edit your video arbitrarily. Each cut from one shot to the next should be both logical and esthetical. It should assist and not hinder the reporter's narration.

A Case History

A student did a story about a veterinarian who was holding classes on how to perform CPR on pets. Her b-roll consisted of a cover shot of her real person with the vet as the narrative informed the audience that HILDA PHILLIPS WANTS TO MAKE SURE SHE'S READY THE NEXT TIME HER DOG DOES SOMETHING STUPID—LIKE EATING A GLASS CHRISTMAS ORNAMENT. On the next sentence, the video cut to a close-up of a stuffed dog that was on the table between the vet and Hilda Phillips as the narration continued: HILDA SAYS HER DOG MOXY IS LIKE FAMILY TO HER. Well, the class broke up and no one heard the rest of the narrative because of the laughter—this woman has a stuffed animal for a pet? Of course the stuffed animal was used to practice CPR on, but because of the edit to the stuffed dog at the precise moment that the reporter was referencing the name of the woman's real dog, the unintentional laugh was inevitable.

EDIT TO THE RHYTHM

There is a rhythm that is set up as a reporter reads his or her narrative. Follow this rhythm when deciding when to cut to the next shot. Most often the rhythm falls on the period at the end of the sentence, or on a pause. Sometimes that's not possible, particularly within the cuts of a sequence, but whenever possible, cutting to the rhythm of the reporter's narrative helps move the video smoothly along without calling abrupt attention to the change of shots.

SUMMARY

Shooting good video is both an art and a craft. Some people have natural ability, but even if you don't, if you follow the rules, your video will look more than acceptable; it will look professional. So shoot steady, shoot sequences, shoot to edit (with the three basic shots, cutaways, and screen direction), and shoot to tell the story.

BOX 11.1 *Visual Critique*

If you can't answer yes to the following questions, your video could be better.

1. **Does the video begin with the most visually interesting shot?**
   Grab the audience off the top. If you're covering a demolition derby, make your opening shot that really great close-up you got when the two junkers collided to the accompanying sound of splintering metal and shattering glass.
   Y____ N ____

2. **Is the visual edited to the rhythm of the reporter's narrative?**
   When your edits complement the reporter's rhythm, the edits appear seamless, natural.
   Y____ N ____

3. **Is there continuity sequencing?**
   Using the three shots—establisher, medium, and close-up—and keeping the axis line in mind ensure that people move naturally without jump cuts and make your video visually appealing and professional.
   Y ____ N____

4. **Does the video effectively utilize the real person to help illustrate the story?**
   The real person should be engaged in action that helps illustrate your story. You have to direct him or her in that action and it should be shot as a continuity sequence. For example, if your story is about a property tax increase, show your real person cutting his grass, tending flowers, and so on, as your voiceover narrative tells the audience about the increase.
   Y ____ N ____

5. **Does your video have natural sound?**
   Always shoot with natural sound. It eliminates unnatural silence while giving ambience and presence to your video.
   Y ____ N ____

6. **Are the interviewees framed head and shoulders only, looking into lead space with proper headroom?**
   Y ____ N____

7. **Do all shots of people have proper headroom and lead space?**
   Headroom and lead space are not just for the interview shot. Always be aware of these elements whenever you are videotaping people.
   Y ____ N ____

8. **Is the reporter either screen left or screen right in the stand-up?**
   The background of the stand-up shot is just as important as the reporter, so the reporter shares the stand-up shot with the background. Giving frame space to the background visually integrates the reporter into the story by putting him or her on the scene.
   Y____ N ____

9. **Does the stand-up have a logical background?**
   Again, the background should integrate the reporter into the story. So there should be some detail. Instead of just a brick wall behind you, move your camera and yourself far enough away from the building to give prominence to both you and the background.
   Y ____ N ____

10. **Is the production free of jump cuts, tilts, pans, and zooms?**
    If any of the aforementioned are part of your video, it probably looks more than just a little amateurish.
    Y ____ N ____

CHAPTER QUIZ

1. The three basic shots that enable continuity sequencing are _____, _____, and _____ .

2. The average length of a shot when edited is _____ to _____ seconds.

3. When you are shooting, each shot should be held for at least _____ seconds.

4. Shooting _____ eliminates jump cuts and compresses real time.

5. Always use a _____ to eliminate shaky shots when shooting.

6. A sequence consists of at least _____ shots.

7. Edit to the _____ of the reporter's narrative.

8. A _____ shot is related to the main action, but takes place in another location.

9. Once you get your real person to cooperate with you in shooting your illustrative b-roll, you should think like a _____ .

10. _____ focus is preferred over _____ focus.

11. You should begin your reporter narrative with your most _____ shot.

12. Your interview shot should be framed with proper _____ and _____ .

13. True or false: You should include plenty of zooms and pans in your production.

14. If movies weren't shot for continuity, actors would _____ all over the screen.

15. Proper screen direction is assured by not crossing the _____ line when shooting action.

16. True or false. It is not necessary for every b-roll shot to include natural sound.

17. Your _____ shot should be your most visually interesting shot.

18. True or false: Your video should avoid isolated shots of signs and building façades.

19. The two standard shots that you will usually get during an office interview are the interview shot and the _____ shot.

20. The _____ cut is the most common edit in a TV news report.

— CHAPTER 12 —

Radio/TV Exercises

USING THE FORMULA WITH WORKBOOK EXERCISES

The following exercises are taken from actual, nonexclusive news events, though names and locations have been changed. In most instances, additional information is created to provide students with those elements necessary to utilize the formula. However, those added elements are of the type that make for good reporting. The information is presented in a random fashion for you to organize via the people-izing formula.

Depending on your instructor's direction, write a radio package (one page only) or a TV package (two pages only) based on the information that makes up the exercises of this chapter. Follow the models given in this book. If you're doing a radio report, be sure that you use only one real person sound bite and one official sound bite. Make sure your real person actuality comes before the official actuality. Be sure to adhere to the requirement of a two-sentence anchor lead (chapter 6) and the suggested number of sentences in the body (chapter 7). If you're doing a TV package, make sure you have two sound bites from your real person and one from your official. Be sure the first sound bite from your real person comes before the official's, and that the second sound bite from your real person comes after the official's (chapter 3). Again, the radio report should be *one* page only and the TV report should be *two* pages only. And remember, *style counts* (chapter 1).

EXERCISE 1

(Note: The information in this exercise may or may not be written in correct broadcast news style. It is up to you to correct it as you script your story. Style counts. Refer to chapter 1.)

The information: Property owners in Our Town are undergoing a citywide property reappraisal that will decide by how much the yearly tax on their homes will increase. Some longtime area residents in a particular neighborhood of Our Town are complaining that it's unfair. They're facing major tax increases. Below are the circumstances and facts you discover after talking with residents and officials at the tax assessor's office.

Real person: Louise Smith, a homeowner in the neighborhood. She tells you:

- Property owners are forming a group to challenge the increased appraisals.
- She faces a 208 percent increase in her property tax, which means she'll pay $500 a year in additional city taxes. She was paying about $240.
- She's owned her home in the Longview Hills subdivision for thirty years.
- Her home is a one-story brick ranch-style with 2,200 square feet and an enclosed carport.
- Her home cost her $32,600 back in 1961.
- The value of her home jumped from $42,700 in the last reappraisal to $123,700 in the current appraisal.

Excerpt the real person actuality or sound bite from the following interview: "My husband and me raised three kids in this house. They're all grown and gone now. Course they never really go; they still visit, bring the grandkids. We spoil those kids rotten, I'll tell you. But this is a good solid neighborhood. People may not be able to afford that $400,000 house that just went up next to them, but they keep up their property and they got a right to stay here and not be gouged for taxes. They keep up their property. I'll tell you it really set me off when a neighbor and me went down there to the tax assessor's office; when we saw what they had down there on land values for us and our neighbors, that did it. The neighborhood is changing slightly, but there are a lot of people that have been here for twenty-five to thirty years. Of course they bought their houses for $30,000 to $40,000, and now all of a sudden they are living in a $230,000, $250,000 house."

Official: Robin Mathews, the county tax assessor. She tells you:

- A number of new and larger houses in the area are now being built and sold for an average of $500,000.
- These new homes are being built as the result of a national phenomenon known as "tear down," where older, smaller homes are being bulldozed by developers, and larger, much more expensive homes of 5,000 square feet are being built.
- Now the value of the land on which these larger homes and smaller homes stand is doubling and even tripling appraisals as the new land sales are being factored into the county computer.
- Smith's neighborhood isn't the only one facing this predicament. At least two other neighborhoods in Our Town—Sycamore View and Lamar Heights—will face similar increases as a result of the developers' "tear down."

Excerpt the official actuality or sound bite from the following interview: "The way we see it, they're buying a property that has an improvement and then tearing down the improvement. So what that means is they really basically just bought the land. We have gotten a number of complaints from homeowners who are really upset. We saw a lot of that in 1998. I just tell them they should consider their house an investment that has increased in value. We may opt, in some instances, to totally disregard the value of the home and tax the owner for just the land it sits on. We try to consider what's fair and to come up with a fair market value, and that's really all we can do."

EXERCISE 2

(Note: The information in this exercise may or may not be written in correct broadcast news style. It is up to you to correct it as you script your story. Style counts. Refer to chapter 1.)

The information: The state's new graduated license law takes effect this week. It requires that a fifteen-year-old who gets a learner's permit enter a three-phase licensing process that won't be completed until age eighteen.

Real person: Mandy Stiles, who is getting her learner's permit, says:

- She recently turned sixteen.
- She's one of many students taking summer driving courses in the Our Town public school system.
- She generally supports the law, but sees some problems.

Excerpt the real person actuality or sound bite from the following interview: "I think it's a good idea and it might reduce car accidents among teenagers 'cause I do think people are driving like fools; they try to show off and I think it should be stopped, but I think it's not right to make teenagers like me wait so long just because we're teenagers. I think a year is just too long; maybe six months."

Official: Ken Darby, a spokesperson for the state Department of Safety. He tells you:

- The law requires more driving practice under adult supervision.
- There's a driving curfew for sixteen-year-olds.
- The law requires more time on the road with a clean driving record before a teenager can receive a regular driver's license.
- The law is basically the state's response to national statistics that showed sixteen-year-olds are three times as likely to have accidents as drivers age eighteen and nineteen, and half again as likely as seventeen-year-olds.

Excerpt the official actuality or sound bite from the following interview: "It does give us some ways to ensure that the drivers that get behind the wheel have all of the experience they need. . . . It also eliminates one possibility of distraction by limiting the number of people in the vehicle unless someone twenty-one or older is in there. Yes, we've gotten some complaints because it's so much different than what we've been doing, but we've also gotten some parents who've called to say thanks, who realize that it's going to be worth it in the long run."

EXERCISE 3

(Note: The information in this exercise may or may not be written in correct broadcast news style. It is up to you to correct it as you script your story. Style counts. Refer to chapter 1.)

The information: Under a new city parking ordinance, the Our Town police department has begun towing cars that violate the time limits on city parking meters. You've received a call from a person whose car was towed, complaining about the $150 towing and storage fee.

Real person: Ron Johnston, whose car was towed. He tells you:

- He had to pay a speeding ticket in traffic court and was only going to be a few minutes.
- He showed up just as his car was being towed away.

Excerpt the real person actuality or sound bite from the following interview: "Man, I couldn't have been expired for more than a minute or so. I was only gone about fifteen minutes, and when I came out the guy already had my car on the truck. I stood in front of the truck, you know; he was going to take my car over my dead body, but he just told me it'll cost you $150 dollars, like that was spare change or something. Man, I don't know how I'm gonna pay that $150."

Official: Roger Smith, chairman of Our Town City Council. He tells you:

- There have been numerous complaints about the new towing policy.
- Booting doesn't work, because the car remains in the parking space, taking up valuable space.
- Prices on the parking meters are reasonable and there is no reason anyone should have a problem paying for meter time.
- Downtown merchants initiated towing because of customers' complaints about the lack of parking spaces.
- He's heard all types of stories and is sympathetic.

Excerpt the official actuality or sound bite from the following interview: "People complain about their cars being towed, but you got people complaining there's no place to park downtown. If we want downtown to be viable, want people to come downtown, then we have to make it possible for them to do so. As for whether the towing fee is excessive, when you add up the administrative cost of towing and add to that the fact that there should be a deterrence element of the ordinance, $150 appears to be about right."

EXERCISE 4

(Note: The information in this exercise may or may not be written in correct broadcast news style. It is up to you to correct it as you script your story. Style counts. Refer to chapter 1.)

The information: The Our Town Police Department formed a special missing persons bureau just over a year ago. You've been assigned to do a story examining its effectiveness during the bureau's first year. The following is the information you find after interviews with your real person and your official.

Real person: Katherine Johns, the mother of eighteen-year-old Christine Johns. She tells you:

- Christine vanished from Our Town on New Year's Day.
- Christine's now been missing about six months.
- She (Katherine) hired private investigators and put up a $5,000 reward.
- No results so far.

Excerpt the real person's actuality or sound bite from the following interview: "I just want to know if she's all right. It was like she just vanished—here one second, gone the next. I'll never stop trying to find her. I know somebody out there knows something."

Official: Will Penny, a police captain and the director of the bureau. He tells you:

- He oversees six police investigators.
- Since the unit went into operation just over a year ago, the officers have cleared 88 percent of their cases.
- The officers work the streets and phones looking for leads. They also distribute flyers and put out descriptions on police broadcast frequencies.
- Alzheimer patients who wander off and juveniles in danger take priority.
- Last month, 387 missing persons or runaway complaints came to the unit. Three hundred and thirty-one have been cleared so far.
- He admits that sometimes, despite all their efforts, nothing seems to work.
- Penny estimates that about half of missing persons cases were cleared before the new unit was formed.

Excerpt the official's actuality or sound bite from the following interview: "Foul play is always a possibility. You never know going in. Once a case comes in, we try to talk to family and friends, try to find out what we can about who last saw the person, what the person was doing before they disappeared. Each case is different. You just don't know before you get the facts. You certainly don't want to jump to conclusions. Warning signs start going off when you can't find a good reason for that person to have gone missing. You develop a kind of sixth sense about these things. We take what we find; we play our hunches. Sometimes we score, sometimes not. [Regarding Christine Johns] We've made all the moves we can make, run the leads as far as they go, hit all the bases, talked with her boyfriend, everyone we could about the day she disappeared. I have to admit it, sometimes you come up empty. You just come up empty."

EXERCISE 5

(Note: The information in this exercise may or may not be written in correct broadcast news style. It is up to you to correct it as you script your story. Style counts. Refer to chapter 1.)

The information: Thirty-one Our Town public schools are on the state's low-performing or "F" list. This has led to a school board crackdown on social promotion. Next year all third, fourth, fifth, and eighth graders who are below grade level must get up to speed during the summer before they can go to the next grade. Cherokee Elementary is on the list and you decide to tell your story using that school.

Real person: Chandra Webb, a fourth grader. She tells you:

- She makes all As.
- She was really upset when she heard her school had made an F in performance.
- She thinks her school is very pretty.

Excerpt the real person actuality or sound bite from the following interview: "I'm embarrassed. We go to a school that has real low grades. They told us we were at the bottom. It makes me feel dumb." [Regarding what she wants to be when she grows up] "I want to work in a pretty building and make lots of money."

Official: Richard Harrison, the principal of Cherokee Elementary. He tells you:

- He is looking for help from the school district's new curriculum and reading programs, which are scheduled for implementation this fall.
- He doesn't expect dramatic improvements in test scores in one year.
- He blames part of the problem on programs aimed at improving academic achievement that didn't take into account the literacy background students need.

Excerpt the official actuality or sound bite from the following interview: "The problem is that children need to learn how to read first. It took three or four years to dig this hole. It will take at least three or four to get out. But at least now we've been thrown a rope. Now maybe our students can begin to climb the ladder of success. I'm very grateful for this new emphasis on reading, because that is what it's all about."

EXERCISE 6

(Note: The information in this exercise may or may not be written in correct broadcast news style. It is up to you to correct it as you script your story. Style counts. Refer to chapter 1.)

The information: There is a new cancer drug being tested. It's called Angiostatin. The company that's developing it, EntreMed Inc., says it's designed to fight cancer without debilitating or even fatal side effects. The drug is still in its testing phase. Tests have shown remarkable cancer regression in mice. The tests are now being done on humans. However, it will be several years before it will be known if the drug will meet expectations.

Real person: Helen Finton, a sixty-three-year-old with cancer. She tells you:

- She's a former schoolteacher, married, and the mother of two.
- Cancer has already been cut from her mouth.
- For the last few months she's eaten by means of her throat; a tube feeds liquid nourishment to her stomach.
- Her doctor thinks the medical team has gotten all her cancer.
- She says it's a scary thing, but if her cancer spreads, she'd volunteer for experimental drug testing.

Excerpt the real person actuality or sound bite from the following interview: "Cancer is not something you'd wish on your worst enemy. Sometimes I think my family suffers more than me. They try not to show it, but the smiles can turn to tears in seconds, especially my kids. They think they got it all. But you can't help thinking about it coming back."

Official: Jim Akins, a doctor who specializes in cancer treatment. He tells you:

- Cancer will kill some 554,000 Americans this year.
- Cancer research is very competitive with forty companies vying for the market.
- It takes seven years for the drugs to go through all the testing stages.

Excerpt the official actuality or sound bite from the following interview: "It's a time-consuming process; development takes so long. It's very emotional. The patients get their hopes up, and then . . . it's like a roller coaster, up and down. Many of the drugs just plain fail. But you know, all the competition, that stimulates the process, too."

EXERCISE 7

(Note: The information in this exercise may or may not be written in correct broadcast news style. It is up to you to correct it as you script your story. Style counts. Refer to chapter 1.)

The information: Kids in Our Town are participating in a new summer community service program known as SAS (Summer After School). The program is designed to give kids something to do in the summer and to make them feel as though they are a part of their communities. You visit the area they're working in, Lamar Terrace, and see them with their brooms, paint cans, mops, and trash bags.

Real person: Lauren Ellis, one of the kids in the program who is helping to clean up and paint. She tells you:

- She is painting Mrs. Frances Boquett's house. She's pretty old.
- She's eleven years old and attends Westside Elementary.
- So far she's swept porches, planted flowers, and painted some steps.

Excerpt the real person actuality or sound bite from the following interview: "I think it's a good program. It makes me happy to see these old houses when we get through with them. I wouldn't be doing anything this summer anyway, so I'm just glad to be helping out 'cause these are real nice people."

Official: Julia Burtrum, the project director. She tells you:

- They have about eighty-five kids helping out.
- They're all elementary school students from Our Town.
- It's a federally funded program operating on a grant of $25,000 for five weeks.
- The kids are earning minimum wage.
- The owners of the houses the kids are working on were visited by members of the SAS staff and asked to participate.
- The kids will visit about thirty houses in several communities before the program ends.

Excerpt the official actuality or sound bite from the following interview: "It's a learning experience for the students. They learn better when they're involved in hands-on projects, and they're getting to know people in their community they might not have ever spoken to before this, and I think when they get to know the community, they have more of a sense of responsibility for it, and that has to be good for everyone."

EXERCISE 8

(Note: The information in this exercise may or may not be written in correct broadcast news style. It is up to you to correct it as you script your story. Style counts. Refer to chapter 1.)

The information: A national survey just released by a nonprofit group, the Alliance for Aging Research, reveals that almost two-thirds of Americans would like to live to be centenarians, that is, live to be one hundred years old. At the same time, the survey found that 63 percent agreed the nation will not have enough hospitals, doctors, and equipment to care for aging baby boomers unless cures are found for major old-age diseases. The survey concludes that most Americans have great expectations for staying healthy and independent.

Real person: Elizabeth Province. She tells you:

- She'd definitely like to live to be one hundred, if she still had reasonably good health.
- She agrees with those in the survey who say that as the population continues to age, there probably won't be enough hospitals for old people.
- She's an Our Town resident.
- She's fifty-two and does telemarketing out of her home.
- She's raised two children, and she has four grandchildren.
- She's never had a serious illness.

Excerpt the real person actuality or sound bite from the following interview: "Well, I had an aunt who lived to be ninety-five and she really seemed to enjoy her life and was in really good shape until her last year where she couldn't get around that well anymore. But her mind was good and she was really an inspiration to me. Yes, I do think that science will develop new things, ways to keep people healthier longer, you know, a way to keep our teeth past seventy."

Official: Dr. Doris Chesterson, who specializes in geriatric treatment. She tells you:

- She's read the article about the survey you gave her and she's not surprised by it.
- No matter what their age or condition, most of her patients want to hold on to life, especially if they have loved ones they care for and who care for them.
- Those who don't seem to have a real interest in continuing to live are those aged patients who seem to be alone—no relatives, few friends.
- Her patients with terminal illnesses, such as cancer, are usually hopeful that a new drug will be found to save them.

Excerpt the official actuality or sound bite from the following interview: "What I've found, in general, is that people want to hang onto life as long as they can, no matter what their age. But I have to qualify that. They want to live if they feel they have reason to and that usually comes down to having interests in life, be that a job, a hobby, friends, relatives, you know, loved ones. What I hear so often from the more sick patients, those who have terminal illness and maybe are in their late seventies or eighties, is: 'I really wouldn't mind dying if it weren't for leaving my wife or my husband or my children, but I know how sad they'll be, and hurt, and I'd like to spare them that.'"

EXERCISE 9

(Note: The information in this exercise may or may not be written in correct broadcast news style. It is up to you to correct it as you script your story. Style counts. Refer to chapter 1.)

The information: The state college board has recommended that salaries for the faculties of the state's universities and community colleges be increased. A survey indicates that at least 160 state faculty members plan to leave the system by the end of the academic year because of inadequate salaries. This is the third year in a row that the faculty will not get a salary increase.

Real person: Dr. George Henderson, an associate professor of biology at Our Town University. He tells you:

- He makes $50,000 a year.
- He's been at Our Town University for fifteen years.
- He and his wife have one child in the sixth grade.
- His last raise was three years ago; it was 5 percent.
- He has accepted a job offer at a university in another state and plans to leave after the current semester.

Excerpt the real person actuality or sound bite from the following interview: "I really don't want to leave. My family and I have been very happy here in Our Town. We like the people and our son hates to have to say good-bye to his friends, but, let's face it, if our teaching were as valued as it should be, we would be fairly compensated and we are not. I've seen the quality of faculty drop in my fifteen years here. If you care for the students, it breaks your heart to see them being deprived of the education they're paying good money for."

Official: Martin Fletcher, the chairman of Our Town University's faculty senate. He tells you:

- Faculty salaries range from a low of about $41,500 to a high of $92,000.
- He says it's impossible to maintain a quality faculty without competitive funding.
- He says Our Town University already has about fifteen professor slots that haven't been filled because of lack of funding, and that about twenty faculty members are expected to leave at the end of the semester for that same reason.

Excerpt the official actuality or sound bite from the following interview: "You know they say the low salaries are the result of the state's current economic woes, but the state is always suffering economic woes, and why is that? I'll tell you, as long as this state continues to ignore education, it will remain a poor state. It will remain at the bottom of the economic ladder. The two are inseparable. We are losing good professors and we are losing the best students and we will continue to lose good people until state lawmakers realize their obligation to this university and to this state."

EXERCISE 10

(Note: The information in this exercise may or may not be written in correct broadcast news style. It is up to you to correct it as you script your story. Style counts. Refer to chapter 1.)

The information: From the Federal Trade Commission's Web page, you learn that identity theft is becoming a national problem. Law enforcement statistics show that some four hundred thousand Americans are affected every year. Thieves gain access to someone's social security number and address, take out credit cards in that person's name, and then charge their purchases to the person from whom they've stolen the social security number.

Real person: Sally Franks, a nurse. She tells you:

- It took her more than five hundred hours and more than $15,000 to clear up the problem caused by the person who stole her identity.
- She lost sleep worrying over it and lost money because she had to take time off work to clear things up.
- She had to call all the credit card companies where things had been charged, and they told her she had to get all her documentation together.
- She's really careful about what information she gives out, so she has no idea how the thieves obtained her information.

Excerpt the real person actuality or sound bite from the following interview: "I got a call from the bank and they said I owed them $11,000. I didn't know what the heck they were talking about. But they had my social security number, my date of birth, and my mother's maiden name. It turned out that someone had charged more than $50,000 in bills to me, including a brand-new Ford SUV. It took forever to clear the mess up."

Official: Earl Smith is a prosecutor with the U.S. attorney's district office in Our Town. He tells you:

- Identity theft is a serious problem, and his office has prosecuted three such cases in the last year.
- What identity thieves do is take your information and create "an evil twin."
- Some pose as telemarketers and solicit information by phone. Others get it directly out of your dumpster. Then they'll call your credit card issuer and, pretending to be you, change the mailing address on your account so you won't be notified of the charges.
- If you become a victim, prepare to spend a lot of time clearing it up.

- The first thing a victim should do is contact the fraud departments of each of the three major credit bureaus and request that a "fraud alert" be placed in his or her file.
- The victim should notify the creditors in writing, close the accounts that have been tampered with, and open new ones with new PIN numbers and passwords.

Excerpt the official actuality or sound bite from the following interview: "A sure way to become a victim is to throw those preapproved credit cards or balance-transfer checks into the garbage without first ripping them up. Don't just say, well, I didn't ask them to send it, and just throw it away, because that's all these dumpster divers need. The main thing is, don't give out personal information unless you're sure of who you're giving it to."

EXERCISE 11

(Note: The information in this exercise may or may not be written in correct broadcast news style. It is up to you to correct it as you script your story. Style counts. Refer to chapter 1.)

The information: Two Our Town teens have died, and their accidental deaths, according to the coroner, were caused by the illegal drug known as Ecstasy. The two did not know each other and took the drug in separate incidents. You've been assigned to do a story about the popularity of this drug and its dangers.

Real person: Clayton Ross. He tells you:

- He's used the drug several times.
- It's pretty cheap, about a dollar a tablet.
- He has never had a problem with it.
- It makes him feel in control.
- None of his friends have ever had any problems.
- He has heard about people OD'ing and about the recent deaths.
- He's heard it depends on what the chemicals are mixed with.

Excerpt the real person actuality or sound bite from the following interview: "I've done it a bunch of times and so have my friends, and I've never seen anybody have any kind of problem with it. It sounds like the cops are trying to scare you away from it 'cause it has become pretty popular. All I know is that anytime I've used it, it's made me feel really in control and pretty sexy."

Official: Bill Preston, an Our Town narcotics detective. He tells you:

- It's the number one recreational drug among teenagers in the nation.
- It's relatively cheap at about a dollar a tablet.
- There have been about fifty arrests so far this year for possession of the drug.
- It is a felony; you can serve time for both possession and distribution.
- He can't talk about the two teens and what happened to them.

Excerpt the official actuality or sound bite from the following interview: "No, we're not trying to scare them away from the drug. What happened to these two kids could happen to any kid who's using the drug. Yes, what chemicals are used to make it can make the difference. But that's just it: you got people all over the place making up this drug in their kitchens, and some of them don't give a damn what they put in it. The thing we'd like those kids who are using it to ask themselves is, 'Do I really know where this came from?' I don't mean who they bought it from. I mean where did it come from? What was it made with? If they don't know the answers to those questions, they could be putting their lives on the line."

EXERCISE 12

(Note: The information in this exercise may or may not be written in correct broadcast news style. It is up to you to correct it as you script your story. Style counts. Refer to chapter 1.)

The information: The seized property of topless-nightclub kingpin Billy Snow is being sold at public auction. The IRS seized the properties and shut them down for being involved in criminal activity. The Internal Revenue Service is auctioning off five of Snow's former properties, including two houses worth a combined estimate of $640,000, the Super Chics topless club for $250,000, Lily's Angels topless club for $164,000, and Snow's former office, set on seven acres in east Our Town. Snow is doing twenty-seven years in Leavenworth Prison for running prostitution, gambling, and money-laundering operations. You attend the auction.

Real person: Jeff Jackson, who bought the Lily's Angels club at the auction. He tells you:

- He says he plans to make it a strip joint again.
- He says he doesn't see any problem with the cops as long as he runs a legitimate business.
- He says topless dancing is legal in Our Town.
- He's a retired policeman.

Excerpt the real person actuality or sound bite from the following interview: "I always wanted to go into business for myself, even while I was a cop. I used to do undercover at Lily's so it'll kind of be like going home. It's legal business here, you know, long as you don't cross the law, so I don't expect I'll have any trouble from the city."

Official: Jerry Parish, a captain with the Our Town police department vice squad. He tells you:

- He was head of the task force that investigated Snow.
- A total of one hundred state, federal, and local law enforcement officials made up the task force.
- It was probably the largest cooperative effort in our state.
- There was a total of $1.3 million in winning bids for the property.

Excerpt the official actuality or sound bite from the following interview: "Yeah, it was some operation, lot of long days and even longer nights, lot of headaches, lot of fun. We got to know the inside of these joints pretty well, undercover work and all. You know, it was like Billy was just asking for it, you know, flaunting the money, the girls, the lifestyle, and I got to say, the guy could really be charming, but I doubt anyone on the business end of his bat would tell you that. But all the stuff you see here, his personal possessions, all that stuff is what it comes down to. I don't know, would you trade twenty-seven years in Leavenworth Penitentiary for that?"

EXERCISE 13

(Note: The information in this exercise may or may not be written in correct broadcast news style. It is up to you to correct it as you script your story. Style counts. Refer to chapter 1.)

The information: Filmmakers from Hollywood are shooting a major movie in Our Town. Shooting has begun on the university campus. The director won't do an interview, but a press release describes the movie as "The story of a young boy's coming of age in a small southern town." They plan to do three days of shooting on the town square. However, the merchants who own the stores on the square are against it. They say closing off the square to accommodate the filmmakers will cost them money in lost business. The movie is scheduled for release around Christmas. The Merchants Association is considering legal action against the Our Town Board of Aldermen to prevent the closure of the square. The chairperson of the Board of Aldermen declined to be interviewed, but she says she's sure the issue can be resolved without going to court.

Real person: Rita Thompson, who has been hired as an extra. She tells you:

- She's in the crowd scene, where they rob the bank on the square.
- She's a theater major at Our Town University.
- She's getting $200 a day.

Excerpt the real person sound bite from the following interview: "I think the business owners are crazy. It's free publicity for them to be seen in a movie. It'll put our little town on the map. I can't wait to see it. I'll probably be hollering, 'That's me, that's me!' every time I pop up. I'm going to add it to my resume. Not everybody can say they've been in a movie with Dennis Hopper."

Official: James Silvers, president of the Our Town Merchants Association. He tells you:

- The Merchants Association estimates that closing the square for the three days of shooting would result in a combined loss of $300,000 in revenues to square merchants.
- Since the story is set in the sixties, the movie's set designers want to change window displays, and even store signs.
- It's not good for customer relations. They don't like to have their shopping days interfered with.

Excerpt the official actuality or sound bite from the following interview: "These Hollywood people just come in here and take over the whole town like they owned it or something. What do they care if we lose money? Yeah, they pay us a little bit for letting them change our signs and such, but it's nothing compared to what we lose. So you get your storefront in a movie with Dennis Hopper. Big deal."

EXERCISE 14

(Note: The information in this exercise may or may not be written in correct broadcast news style. It is up to you to correct it as you script your story. Style counts. Refer to chapter 1.)

The information: A student from Our Town University has been hospitalized after crashing his SUV through the security gate of the Federal Building located in Our Town. The incident happened in the early morning hours. The student is under arrest, but federal officials won't say what he's been charged with. Friends say he threatened suicide shortly before he drove his vehicle through the gate.

Real person: Joyce Boon, a friend of the student. She tells you:

- He's been real upset because he didn't get into the fraternity he wanted.
- He's really a nice guy, very smart.
- She's known him since their freshman year in high school.

Excerpt the real person actuality or sound bite from the following interview: "I tried to tell him that it was their loss, not his, that he didn't get in that fraternity. I know he was seeing a counselor at the university Wellness Center. I guess it didn't help. I can't imagine why he would have been at the Federal Building."

Official: Charles Lawrence, who is the FBI Agent in Charge at the Federal Building. He tells you:

- The name of the student is not being released at this time.
- The incident is still under investigation.
- No comment on what the student intended to do after crashing the gate, or why he was at the Federal Building.
- Damage to the gate is approximately $3,000.
- No comment on whether he's been charged with a crime.
- An arraignment has been set for tomorrow morning in federal court.

Excerpt the official actuality or sound bite from the following interview: "The FBI does consider this a serious breach of security. No violation of this type is taken lightly, not since the Oklahoma bombing. We are still investigating. We do understand he has been undergoing counseling for mental depression. No, I don't want to speculate at this time on what he may or may not be charged with."

EXERCISE 15

(Note: The information in this exercise may or may not be written in correct broadcast news style. It is up to you to correct it as you script your story. Style counts. Refer to chapter 1.)

The information: Our Town police dispatchers are attending Spanish classes. They are learning the language in order to communicate with the increasing number of Spanish-speaking residents who are coming from Mexico to work construction jobs at the university and in the city.

Real person: Darlene Snapple, an Our Town police dispatcher. She tells you:

- She's been a dispatcher with the Our Town police department for two years.
- She took Spanish in high school but doesn't remember much.
- She's taking lessons in a special class being held at the Our Town University.
- They're learning just enough to be able to communicate.

Excerpt the real person actuality or sound bite from the following interview: "If we get a call from a hysterical Spanish-speaking person, we can calm them down. We can ask if they need a police officer, or if they need an ambulance or the fire department. It helps to talk to someone when they call, and if they don't speak English, we can't help. Now we can speak a little bit of their language and find out what's going on."

Official: Larry Woods, Our Town police captain. He tells you:

- He doesn't expect the dispatchers to become fluent from the short course they are taking.
- It's a two-day course.
- It's mandatory for the dispatchers.
- There are four dispatchers in the Our Town police department.

Excerpt the official actuality or sound bite from the following interview: "We have so many Spanish-speaking people coming into Our Town to work construction jobs, with the town growing like it is, that we have to be able to communicate with them, because they have the same problems and emergencies as anybody else. With this course, our dispatchers will at least be able to get some form of communication across."

EXERCISE 16

(Note: The information in this exercise may or may not be written in correct broadcast news style. It is up to you to correct it as you script your story. Style counts. Refer to chapter 1.)

The information: An official with the Our Town Animal Shelter has called you to ask your assistance in publicizing a problem that recurs every summer. It seems the stray animal population in Our Town increases as the student population decreases. In other words, students leaving Our Town University for the summer are not taking their adopted pets home with them. Instead they are letting them go on the streets of Our Town, resulting in the annual summer increase in stray animals.

Real person: Maggie Farmer, a university student with a pet cat. She tells you:

- She got Cynthia from the pound.
- She's had Cynthia for four months.
- She's a freshman.
- It helps to have a pet around to take your mind off yourself when you start feeling lonesome and homesick.

Excerpt your real person actuality or sound bite from the following interview: "I love her to death, but if my parents told me I couldn't bring her home with me, I'd probably let her go if I couldn't find somebody to take her. If I hadn't adopted her to begin with, the animal shelter would have put her to sleep. They do that after three days, I think. So I wouldn't want to take her back because she's older now and probably nobody else would adopt her, and they'd put her to sleep and it would be my fault. I just wish the shelter didn't have to put them to sleep."

Official: Mary Ann Chaney, the director of the Our Town Animal Shelter. She tells you:

- The stray animal population increases by thirty percent every summer.
- Most of that increase is because of homebound university students releasing their pets.
- The shelter routinely puts animals to sleep after a week if they aren't claimed or adopted.

Excerpt the official actuality or sound bite from the following interview: "Yes, we do have to put animals to sleep on a regular basis, and even more so in the summer. But it's more humane than leaving them to fend for themselves. These have been pets, used to being inside, being cared for; then they're put out on their own. You wouldn't believe the shape some of these animals are in by the time they wind up here, and sooner or later they do. They come in coated with fleas; they have mange. We've had them come in with bullet wounds; people shoot at them. These students need to know they're not doing their pets a favor by letting them go rather than bringing them back to the shelter."

EXERCISE 17

(Note: The information in this exercise may or may not be written in correct broadcast news style. It is up to you to correct it as you script your story. Style counts. Refer to chapter 1.)

The information: The federal government plans to quit minting pennies under the Legal Tender Modernization Act. The act is designed to cut down on wasteful production. Because so many people hoard pennies rather than keep them in circulation, according to federal officials, the U.S. Mint had to produce 14.3 billion of them last year. They say two-thirds of existing pennies are not in circulation. They're in places like piggy banks and wishing wells.

Real person: Trevor Langston, a person who doesn't spend his pennies. He tells you:

- Pennies are a nuisance.
- He puts them in a giant plastic whisky display bottle he got from a liquor store.
- He figures he has about $100 in pennies.
- You have to put them in those wrappers before the bank will cash them in.

Excerpt the real person actuality or sound bite from the following interview: "I've filled the bottle before, so I know about how full it has to get to reach a hundred dollars, but I don't know if I'll cash them in this time. It's not easy stuffing those pennies into the wrapper. You get them crossways; then you have to start all over again, and you lose count. It's not worth the aggravation. I wish stores would just figure their prices so that when tax is included, everything just comes out even, and then they don't have to give you any change."

Official: Van Marcoby, an economics professor at Our Town University. He tells you:

- Some argue that the elimination of pennies from cash registers would save consumers and retailers time and money.
- Proponents say pennies could be eliminated by legalizing the rounding up or down to the nearest nickel on cash transactions.
- Studies show most Americans would like to eliminate pennies and have prices rounded to the nearest nickel. But penny backers say rounding would lead to widespread overcharges.

Excerpt the official actuality or sound bite from the following interview: "Other nations, including France, Spain, and Britain, have stopped producing their coins of low denomination. That's because of the coins' low purchasing power and the increasing costs of minting them. The U.S. has tried this before, you know, making it legal to round off the cost of things to eliminate the penny, but opponents say merchants would round things upward, and that would create a de facto tax on the poor who conduct more transactions in cash. In fact, there was one study that said rounding would cost consumers something like six hundred million dollars a year. If I had to guess, I'd say it's not going to happen anytime soon."

EXERCISE 18

(Note: The information in this exercise may or may not be written in correct broadcast news style. It is up to you to correct it as you script your story. Style counts. Refer to chapter 1.)

The information: It's summer and children will soon be swimming. The Consumer Product Safety Commission is concerned about the dangers children face in home pools. The CPSC reports that over 350 children drown in home pool accidents each year. The CPSC news release contains the following safety tips: designate a child watcher when you attend a party or have friends or family over; talk with baby-sitters about pool safety; don't rely on swimming lessons or "floaties" to protect your children in the water; and post rules such as "No running" and "Never swim alone." Your news director wants you to do a story on safety tips for parents of young children with access to home pools.

Real person: Tom Provosty, the father of a young child. He tells you:

- Crissy is six years old.
- She's attending swimming classes at Our Town University.
- He knows how to do CPR.
- He plans to install a home pool.

Excerpt the real person actuality or sound bite from the following interview: "Crissy's been taking lessons for about three weeks now. Her mother or I are always with her. I'll stand near the pool and watch her in case I have to make a running leap, lifeguard or no, because I know they've got a lot of kids to watch and I can't be sure they'll be looking in my kid's direction if she gets in trouble. I think too many parents take this kind of thing for granted and think they don't have to worry because it's school sponsored or something, and somebody else will look out for their child. I think that's crazy."

Official: Elaine Overton, a lifeguard for Our Town University pool. She tells you:

- Some parents stay with their children; some don't.
- She's probably saved at least four kids in her two years as lifeguard at the university pool.

Excerpt the official actuality or sound bite from the following interview: "I'm amazed at how little parents know about even the basic rules about pool safety, and I'm talking about parents who have pools at their houses. My experience is that most parents don't even know how to give CPR or first aid. My advice to those parents is learn CPR; you could be sorry if you don't."

SUMMARY

Look for the elements that are found in these story exercises in every story you do. Use the formula as defined in this workbook. No, you don't want to become a simple formulaic writer, just plugging in the parts where they go to fit the whole. But, yes, you do want to be aware of structure, of how elements fit together. The formula is designed to guide you into thinking about what constitutes a story, a human story, a people-ized story. Where you go from here depends on how sincerely you want to communicate with people.

CHAPTER 13

Video Exercises

JUST DOING IT

The exercises in this chapter are designed to help make you comfortable with the shooting and editing process before you begin actually shooting news video. Most consumer-grade camcorders are more than adequate for your purposes. If you or your school has access to video editing software, become familiar with the fundamentals of nonlinear editing by using the software's help menu and tutor. Do the same with the camera you'll be using. Keep its manual handy. The more you know about your equipment, the fewer surprises you'll have to deal with. Even though cameras and tripods have become smaller and lighter, you'll find that the logistics of getting from here to there to shoot your interviews and b-roll can be quite exhausting. However, if you don't find it exhilarating and rewarding at the same time, again, that's when you should begin thinking about a new major.

EXERCISE 1

The Talking Head/Over-the-Shoulder Sequence

The interview with the official in an office setting is one of the most common elements of a TV news report. The person being interviewed is often referred to in broadcast news jargon as a *talking head*. That's because the head shot dominates the frame. This shot is also referred to as a *head-and-shoulders* shot because a bit of the shoulders is also a part of the framed composition (see Figure 11.1).

When doing an office interview, a setup shot is included. This is called the *over-the-shoulder* shot. It is a two-shot in which the person being interviewed is framed over the shoulder of the reporter. The shot includes the back of the reporter's head, his or her shoulder, and the interviewee facing the camera and looking at the reporter (see figure 11.2). The shot serves two functions. It helps locate the two in relationship to each other, and it gives the reporter a good five seconds' worth of video for voiceover narration, if needed, within the overall story. The over-the-shoulder shot should be videotaped while the reporter is engaged in small talk with the interviewee before the actual interview begins.

Your camera and tripod should remain in the *same place for each shot*. In other words, don't shoot your over-the-shoulder shot, then physically move your camera to another spot in the office. Frame your over-the-shoulder shot so that you can simply zoom in and frame the interview shot from the same position.

Your edited exercise will include the two shots listed below preceded by a countdown.

1. The countdown: should start on the number 6 and will precede all of the exercises you do.

2. The over-the-shoulder shot: should be at least ten seconds and should approximate the demonstration conducted in lab class, including natural-sound audio.

3. The interview shot: should be at least ten seconds long. It should approximate the demonstration conducted in lab class, including the audio of the official talking.

Your official should be someone other than yourself, as should your reporter. Use friends.

Your video must be shot with a tripod and include natural sound, and your edited production should begin with a countdown.

EXERCISE 2

The Stand-up

The stand-up is that place in a packaged story wherein the reporter gets to take credit for the report she is doing. This is the place the reporter's face hangs out. This is the place you want to make the reporter look good so that she has visual credibility. That means the reporter has to have *presence*. The videographer is very important in making that happen. The way the videographer frames the reporter can make all the difference between a reporter who looks small and not very authoritative and one who looks forceful and confident.

Your assignment is to shoot a reporter stand-up in front of a building. It should not be the one used in the class demonstration, but the reporter should be similarly framed so that the façade of the building is recognizable (see figure 11.3). The stand-up should be at least fifteen seconds long, one shot only, and the audio should be crisp and clear. You will use someone other than yourself to play the part of the reporter. This will be a stationary rather than a walking stand-up.

As always, your video must be shot with a tripod and include natural sound, and your edited production should begin with a countdown.

EXERCISE 3

The Wastebasket Sequence

You will duplicate the sequence shot in class of a person sitting at a desk reading a letter-sized note with which the person becomes so disgusted that he or she wads the paper up and throws it into a wastebasket across the desk.

You will edit the sequence in such a manner that it looks as though the action takes place in real time. The sequence must include natural sound and be composed of the following six shots only in the following order:

1. Establisher of person sitting at the desk reading the note.

2. Close-up of the person's face as he or she reads the note, then starts to wad the paper.

3. Close-up of the note being wadded.

4. Establisher of the person throwing the wadded note toward the wastebasket and out of the frame.

5. Close-up of the paper landing in the wastebasket. (Remember screen direction and make sure the wadded paper comes from the proper direction—don't cross the axis line.)

6. Establisher of the person giving the camera a thumbs-up.

As always, your video must be shot with a tripod and include natural sound, and your edited production should begin with a countdown.

EXERCISE 4

The Computer Sequence

You will duplicate the sequence shot in class of a person walking into a room, taking a seat at a computer, and typing. All shots must be shot on tripod.

Your finished production will consist of the following six shots only, in the order listed, complete with natural sound:

1. Medium shot of the person coming through the door, walking toward the camera and to the side of it, not *crossing* in front of the camera.

2. Establisher of the computer and desk from a *side angle,* and then of the person entering and taking a seat.

3. Close-up of the person's face in profile as he or she types.

4. Close-up of the person's hands typing on the keys.

5. Over-the-shoulder of the person that includes the computer screen as he or she types.

6. Close-up of the screen from the person's point of view.

As always, your video must be shot with a tripod and include natural sound, and your edited production should begin with a countdown.

EXERCISE 5

The Food Court Sequence

This is an exercise in which you get a stranger (a real person) to cooperate with you. You will shoot a sequence in the fast-food area of the student union or cafeteria in which a student buys lunch. The sequence will include natural sound and a sound bite. You must use a tripod. Your sequence will consist of the following nine shots *only*, in the following order:

1. Establisher of student deciding on and selecting the last item for his or her lunch.

2. Close-up of item being placed on tray. The tray should show the other items that have already been selected. You should hold the shot until the person's hands grip the tray in preparation for picking it up and walking away with it.

3. Medium shot of person as he or she lifts the tray off the tray rail and walks out of the frame.

4. Close-up of money or card being handed to the clerk.

5. Close-up from the person's point of view of the price being registered.

6. Medium shot of the clerk and the person as the clerk gives back card or change.

7. Establisher of table as the person walks into the frame and starts to sit the tray on the table.

8. Close-up of the tray as it is placed on the table as person sits down.

9. Interview shot wherein you ask your real person what she thinks of the food court food. The sound bite should be framed with the proper lead space as though the person is talking to an off-camera reporter after sitting at the table. Make sure you do not cross the axis line when shooting the interview. In other words, the person should not appear to have jumped across the table from where she sat down, but should continue to look in the same direction in which she sat. Your sound bite should be at least ten seconds long.

As always, your video must be shot with a tripod and include natural sound, and your edited production should begin with a countdown.

EXERCISE 6

The Drink of Water Sequence

In this exercise you will videotape a person walking into the kitchen, getting a drink of water, and leaving.

Since the exercise is designed to demonstrate your understanding of how to use the three shots (establisher, medium, close-up) that go into creating a *continuity sequence,* you will not be instructed as to which of the three framings to use for each of the shots listed below, though you will *only* use the six shots listed below, in the following order:

1. Person enters kitchen through a doorway in such a manner that we know the person is walking into a kitchen (we see a fridge, cabinets, etc.)

2. Person gets glass from shelf.

3. Person gets water from faucet.

4. Person drinks water.

5. Person sets glass on counter.

6. Person exits the kitchen.

It will be your job to avoid *jump cuts* by using a combination of the three standard shots and their variations that we have learned in class. In other words, you will adapt what you have learned from your previous exercises.

Do not add shots to those listed here, do not combine shots, do not omit shots, and do not rearrange the order of the shots.

As always, your video must be shot with a tripod and include natural sound, and your edited production should begin with a countdown.

EXERCISE 7

The Music Video

You will shoot and edit a 1:30 (it can be longer if you want) video based on a music selection of your choice. The video will illustrate the tune you select and be based on your interpretation of the song. The purpose of this exercise is to enhance your understanding of how the audio and video tracks work together to form an esthetic whole. It is also designed to stimulate your creativity in the editing process. Your production should:

1. Follow both the lyric and the beat of the song.

2. Include at least three continuity sequences composed of a good mixture of cover, medium, and close-up shots that incorporate what you've learned about continuity sequencing.

3. Since this is a music video, you may also break the rules to some extent. In other words, if it is clear that what you are doing is intentional, for effect, you may use jump cuts, cross the axis line, and use whatever effects are available in the editing software or in the digital camera. But, again, it is required that you have at least three standard continuity sequences.

Since this is a music video, you will not be restricted to a tripod or even to the use of natural sound.

SUMMARY

Once you get into shooting and editing, your viewing habits will change. You'll find yourself a critic of every movie, every TV show, and every newscast you watch. You'll be looking for proper headroom and lead space. A jump cut or unexpected change in screen direction will jar you. You'll bore your friends with your observations. But these are all signs that you love what you're doing, and that can't be bad.

CHAPTER 14

Topics for Reporting Your Own Stories

STORIES ARE ALL AROUND YOU

Why do you watch the news? What makes the stories on the evening newscast worth watching? What makes a story newsworthy? If you can answer the first question, you probably have your answer to the second and third. A percentage of the stories we see on the news are those stories journalists feel we need to know to be informed citizens. Those stories mainly deal with federal, state, and local governments, including the courts and law enforcement. But even in such stories, it still comes down to the one thing all stories share in common—they are always fundamentally about *people*. So we're back where we started. Stories are all around you, because *people* are all around you.

A Case History

Remember that story about the adopted puppy that got sick shortly after being brought home from the animal shelter? How did that story come about? Basically because of the student reporter's curiosity. She had simply asked her friend how he was enjoying his new pet. That was how she learned the puppy had developed distemper the week the friend brought it home from the shelter. The friend had paid the required fees, which he assumed ensured not only the spaying of the animal but also its general health. As she talked with her friend, the student reporter learned the puppy's illness had caused her friend not only some concern, but also about $400 in vet fees. That didn't seem quite fair to the student reporter, and she decided to find out the shelter's policy concerning the health issues of the animals it offered for adoption. As we saw earlier, her curiosity resulted in a story with the following anchor lead: IF YOU'RE LOOKING TO ADOPT A PET, OUR TOWN ANIMAL SHELTER HAS A NUMBER TO CHOOSE FROM. BUT AS HOPE WALKER REPORTS, THERE ARE THINGS YOU SHOULD KNOW REGARDING THE HEALTH OF ADOPTED ANIMALS.

Using her friend as the real person, the student reporter constructed an informative story for her audience. In it, we learned that the shelter houses animals no matter what their condition of health, that viruses are always a risk in tight quarters, and that while officials make every effort to be sure pets are in good health when offered for adoption, occasionally one with health problems will slip through. We also learned that the reporter's friend could have saved himself $400 if he'd been aware of the shelter's policy of paying for medical treatment in the event that the pet became sick during the first week of adoption. Newsworthy? You bet.

Another student was getting his annual dental checkup. As he sat in the chair, he noticed the informational literature on the wall regarding tongue rings. The professionals advised against them. The literature talked of cracked teeth, infections, and worn gums from the nervous rubbing of rings against the gum line. An informational story complete with healthy how-to tips for those already wearing tongue rings grew out of this simple office literature and the fact that the student reporter was alert to the simple fact that stories *are all around you.*

CAMPUS STORIES

Look around your university. Your campus is rife with issues. Sexually transmitted diseases, STDs, are a major concern of campus health officials. What are they doing to educate students? Crime: Does your university police department have a Web site? It's a good source for story ideas. How common is vandalism? Date rape? Sexual assault? What programs are campus cops using to ensure safety on your campus? Drugs: What's the drug of choice on your campus, according to police officials? How many drug arrests were made last semester? DUIs: Are they common on your campus? What programs does your school have in place to educate students about responsible drinking? Clubs: Are there any unusual clubs that would make good feature stories? Gun club? Fencing club? Foreign-movie club? Volunteer organizations? A Habitat for Humanity chapter? Perhaps it needs more volunteers. That would be a good angle for a feature story. Is your university involved in research of any kind? Would that research project interest your audience? Does your university Web site have an expert page (a list of professors who are experts on certain subjects)? You might find your idea for a story and your official on the same page.

COMMUNITY STORIES

Read your community newspaper. Attend city board meetings. Develop beats—fire, police, and city council. Look around you as you walk or drive to school. A student reporter passed the long-abandoned and run-down train station along his route to school every day. What would become of it, he wondered. He contacted the local historic preservation society. His subsequent story not only included some very interesting history about the station (university students had departed from the station for the Civil War in 1861) but also revealed that the society definitely thought the old train station was worth saving, though resources were limited and the society had more pressing concerns at the moment. Those other concerns could also make for good stories.

READ

Read national periodicals such as *Time*, *Newsweek*, and even *Rolling Stone*. Read local and national newspapers. These are good sources of information that can inspire you to produce your own *localized* reports. For instance, a student read a *Time* magazine article about the removal of peanut butter from several school lunch programs across the country because some students had adverse reactions to peanut butter. The student checked to see what the school system in Our Town was doing about the popular sandwich spread. He found that local schools had received phone calls from concerned parents, but had decided not to remove peanut butter from the school menu. That formed the basis of his localized report on this issue.

LOCATING YOUR REAL PERSON

As we've seen in the previous example of the pet adoption story, sometimes the real person can be the stimulus for the story. Had the student reporter not talked with her friend about his new pet, she would not have become curious about the health issue.

Often your official can help in lining up a real person who's had experience with the story you plan to cover. For example, if you're doing a story on the new childbirthing class being offered by a local hospital, the person conducting the class would be able to put you in touch with the real person of that story—a class participant. You would simply ask the instructor to canvass the class for anyone interested in participating in the story. The official would probably be happy to help out in light of the positive publicity your story would bring to the hospital as well as to the class.

Sometimes just plain knocking on doors is the only way to find your real person. That can sometimes be time consuming, but also well worth the effort.

A Case History

A student was doing a story about possible groundwater contamination around a rural dumpsite in the county. In addition to the fact that houses were somewhat spread out, the residents were poor and suspicious of strangers. Our student spent several hours walking and driving from door to door in the rain. At her fourteenth house she found a resident willing to talk with her. It was time well spent, as that resident not only added the human touch to the story, but also provided much of the necessary illustrative video (a dumpsite alone can get pretty boring). The student videotaped a sequence of the man entering his house and getting a drink of water from the kitchen faucet. She combined that with a sound bite about his feelings about drinking the water from his kitchen tap.

That story should make it clear that reporting requires not only persistence but also the ability to persuade people to cooperate with you.

Persuading someone to do what you want him or her to do often requires putting your-self in that person's shoes. What would it take to get you to cooperate? If you can persuade the person that it would benefit the community at large, you're more than halfway home. People really do like to help others if they can. And, in fact, if your story is worth doing, it will benefit those in your audience to some degree.

SUMMARY

There are those news days when stories are breaking left and right. There's a bank robbery on the west side of town, a city official has just been indicted for malfeasance, and a major fire has broken out downtown. But there are more days when there really doesn't seem to be much going on. That's where your curiosity comes in. You're in a field that allows you to satisfy your curiosity. Exercise it; get curious about your environment. Look around your college, your community—any number of stories are there waiting to be told. When you find your story, quite often you will find a real person associated with it. If not, ask the official of your story; frequently he or she can steer you in the right direction. Then exercise your powers of persuasion to get that real person to help you make your story the best it can be.

CHAPTER QUIZ

1. Aside from sports, what's the hottest issue on your campus at the moment?

2. Would this story interest your news audience?

3. Why?

4. Who would you interview as the official of that story?

5. Who would be the real person of the story?

6. How would you locate him or her?

7. List seven questions you would ask the real person of your story.

8. List seven questions you would ask the official.

9. List the facts you would expect to include in this story.

10. How would you use the real person to illustrate this story?

CHAPTER 15

Computer-Assisted Reporting

YOU ALREADY KNOW HOW

If you've ever searched the Internet for a favorite song, information on a favorite singer or movie star, or the e-mail address of a friend from another college, you've done a variation of computer-assisted reporting. In doing so, you realized that information is truly at your fingertips. As Mike Wendland wrote in the third edition of *Wired Journalist: Newsroom Guide to the Internet*, "There's nothing magical or mystical about the Net: Like the telephone, the fax machine and the pager, it's just another tool that makes it easier to do our jobs."

E-MAIL

Let's start with e-mail. You've tried several times by phone without success to contact the official you need for your story. Why didn't you think of it before? E-mail her. In a few sentences tell her what your story is about, what you'd like to ask her. Leave her your schedule and find out hers. A search tool known as "Switchboard" is a good source for finding e-mail addresses. Find Switchboard at www.switchboard.com.

SEARCH ENGINES

Raise your hand if you've ever used a search engine. They're nothing new, right? Right. But as a reporter, you have a new use for them.

A Case History

The annual pumpkin patch of a local church attracted the attention of a student reporter. He decided to do a feature on the church and the thousands of pumpkins that fill the lawns surrounding the church every year. The student was unsuccessful in contacting a church representative, and the person selling the pumpkins wasn't much help. So what was he going to do to make his story interesting? He decided to go online. He chose the search engine Google, typed in the single word "pumpkin," and came up with several listings. At the top of the list was:

> University of Illinois Extension, Pumpkin History. Pumpkin Facts. Varieties, Growing Pumpkins, Nutrition, Selection Uses, Description, Pumpkin farms, pumpkin nutrition, varieties and selection, and fun activities for children.

It proved to be just what the student reporter needed. Armed with the Internet information, he decided to change his approach to the story. The church's pumpkin patch would still figure in his report, but would no longer be the focus of it. The new focus would be on the pumpkin itself. The student felt he had enough to prepare an entertaining feature story about pumpkins, and he could use the church's pumpkin patch to illustrate it. Was he right? Decide for yourself.

ACR: GLOWING PUMPKIN FACES WILL SOON BE GREETING KIDS ON DOOR STOOPS AROUND THE COUNTRY AS HALLOWEEN ROLLS AROUND ONCE AGAIN. DAVE HOTARD TELLS US HOW THE PUMPKIN BECAME A JACK-O-LANTERN, AS WELL AS OTHER LITTLE KNOWN PUMPKIN FACTS.

V: DID YOU KNOW THE FIRST JACK-O-LANTERNS WEREN'T MADE OUT OF PUMPKINS? SEVEN-YEAR-OLD B-J BAINS WAS SURPRISED TO LEARN THAT. WE TALKED TO HIM AS HE AND HIS PARENTS WERE PUMPKIN SHOPPING AT ST. PETER'S EPISCOPAL'S ANNUAL PUMPKIN PATCH. B-J WAS EVEN MORE SURPRISED TO LEARN WHAT JACK-O-LANTERNS WERE ORIGINALLY MADE OUT OF—RUTABAGAS, POTATOES, OR TURNIPS—EVEN BEETS.

ACTUALITY: B. J. Bains, pumpkin lover.

Beets!

V: THE UNIVERSITY OF ILLINOIS EXTENSION SERVICE SAYS THE ANCIENT CELTICS USED GOURDS TO CARRY EMBERS FOR BUILDING THEIR

HALLOWEEN BONFIRES. SO FROM A BEET TO A GOURD TO A PUMPKIN. BASIL RICHARDS OVERSEES THE ST. PETER'S EPISCOPAL PUMPKIN PATCH. HE SAYS THERE'S JUST SOMETHING ABOUT PUMPKINS PEOPLE LIKE.

ACTUALITY: Basil Richards, St. Peter's Episcopal.

Sunday, within thirty minutes after we unloaded them, somebody had brought a two-month-old baby by to lay him in the pumpkins and take pictures.

V: HERE'S SOMETHING ELSE B-J DIDN'T KNOW. PUMPKINS WERE ONCE USED FOR REMOVING FRECKLES AND TREATING SNAKEBITES, AND ONE PUMPKIN CAN WEIGH UP TO A THOUSAND POUNDS. DAVE HOTARD, W-X-X-X NEWS.

As the pumpkin story makes clear, search engines can instantly find the topic you're looking for. Had our student punched in the word "beets" or "rutabagas," he would have no doubt found all he ever wanted to know about those subjects.

JOURNALISTS' ONLINE HELP

There are a number of organizations online to help guide journalists in searching out information on the Internet. One of the best is the Journalist's Toolbox. This free site contains more than 2,800 links designed to aid professional, college, and high school journalists. The Web site includes the following topics: Global journalism, visual/design journalism, journalism organizations, broadcasting, journalism jobs and internships, photojournalism, Web editing tools, copy editing, and writing. Find the Journalist's Toolbox at www.journaliststoolbox.com.

Other sites for journalists include:

- Investigative Reporters and Editors, Inc.: www.ire.org
- National Institute for Computer-Assisted Reporting: www.nicar.org
- The Poynter Institute: www.poynter.org
- The Reporters Committee for Freedom of the Press: www.rcfp.org

And of course you can always use search engines like Google to find even more.

A WORD OF WARNING

The fact that the information is on the Net does not make it true. Always look for the source of the information. In our student's case, there would have been no earth-shattering consequences if some of his information about pumpkins wasn't correct. But the last thing a reporter wants shattered is his or her credibility. Always check out the source of your Internet information. For example, the pumpkin information came from the University of Illinois Extension Service. Legitimate sites include an address other than an e-mail address or post office box. Legitimate sites also include a person to contact and a telephone number. And always look for attribution.

SUMMARY

The Internet can save you time when gathering information for a story and can even inspire story ideas. It's a good place to gather facts. Just be sure the facts you gather are facts before you pass them on to your news audience.

CHAPTER QUIZ

Find information on your favorite singer or movie star on the Internet. Use the bio information you find to structure a radio or TV news story about the entertainer. You should be able to find actualities or sound bites at some sites. Incorporate those into a radio report or even a TV report. You should follow the people-ized approach in structuring your story. Find a fan to comment on your star and use that fan as your real person. A record producer, movie director, or entertainment critic could provide your official comment. Just be sure you attribute all of your information.

CHAPTER 16

Convergence and Online Journalism

TRIAL BY FIRE

On the early morning of August 27, 2004, a deadly fire erupted at the Alpha Tau Omega fraternity house on the campus of the University of Mississippi. It was the first day of classes for the fall semester. Coincidentally, it was the first semester of the S. Gale Denley Student Media center's new convergence operation. The day of the fire was also the first time many of the center's students had entered the newly renovated facility, which now housed the center's transplanted newspaper, TV and radio stations, and online operation, together for the first time after occupying separate spaces in Farley Hall. "The number of students grew as they heard about the story, around eighty to ninety students over the course of the day. Some of the journalism professors brought their entire class to see how they could help," recounts Traci Mitchell, the SMC's assistant director. "We put a bunch of people to work who had never done anything for Student Media. Everyone just did whatever it took to get the information out to the public. We had students step up to make key decisions in broadcasting live news briefs [on both TV and radio], streaming video on the Web site, and it all centered around the [convergence] desk right here. We had Joy Douglas who was doing online updates as they came in. We were surrounding her because she needed a lot of stuff, go get me this, go get me that, and people just go and get it."

This trial by fire convinced those working at the Student Media Center that convergence is not an ephemeral concept, that it can be a practical and expedient means of delivering the news in the new millennium. Still, they share the reservations of many professionals when it comes to the routine practicality of the converged news operation.

THE ECONOMICS OF CHANGE

Convergence and online journalism are the new frontiers of journalism. Simply stated, convergence is the marrying of three very separate and distinct journalistic disciplines—broadcast, print, and online. It becomes possible when a company owns more than one media outlet in a local or national market. According to a study entitled *The Convergence Continuum: A Model for Studying Collaboration Between Media Newsrooms* conducted by faculty of Ball State University, these "relationships became more attractive as declining or flat circulation numbers forced newspapers to look for new ways to market their product to the younger audiences television news sometimes attracts,[1] and budget cuts at many television stations required news directors to push staff productivity to the limits."

The Pew Research Center states in a 2004 study that the percentage of those Americans who get their news from the Internet has increased steadily over the past four years. The study reveals that the number of people who go online for news at least three days a week has grown from 23 percent in 2000 to 29 percent by 2004. According to Journalism.org's *The State of the News Media 2004* annual report on American journalism, many Web sites have now reached a point where they can claim profitability, though the money being made on the Internet remains a relatively small part of company income. The report goes on to state that it will be years before the Internet actually pays for the journalism it produces rather than piggybacking off the parent source. SMC director and broadcast journalism professor Dr. Ralph Braseth says that's typical of both broadcast and print, especially newspapers. "What's passing for convergence right now is they take their newspaper and they upload it to the Web and there's not really a heck of a lot of difference." Braseth has spent time at a "multi-media boot camp" sponsored by the University of North Carolina at Chapel Hill, and has studied the best convergence programs at the nation's prominent journalism schools, where, as the *Convergence Continuum* reports,

> "This one-does-all approach often is seen as synonymous with multimedia journalism or new media journalism.[2] In some cases, writers have suggested journalists will go into the field with a miniature, computer-based workstation that allows them to record their notes electronically, research databases, capture visual images, and write their stories.[3] In the academy, this process is described as preparing students to provide information for print, audio, video, or online media or some com-

bination of those media. That approach to convergence is espoused on campuses at such schools as the universities of Kansas and Florida.[4] Students at those schools learn how to craft news stories for print media as well as how to edit audio and/or video files and produce databases of information. At Brigham Young University, integrated media training has become more important and faculty members say students who possess skills that span across several media are more valued than those students who specialize.[5]

Still, Braseth says, "It's so understudied, so much anecdotal stuff, and it's so emotional, and it's so threatening to those of us who have been in the business or are in it—we don't have a lot of hard information."

The driving force behind the move toward convergence appears to be money. All agree that advertising will benefit three ways, selling to separate audiences in print, online, and broadcast media. However, some say it may not work as well for the overall quality of journalism itself. To some, the advances in computerized media mean that separate reporters will no longer be needed for newspaper, TV station, and Web site. The story will be covered only once and the same reporter will file to all three outlets. Braseth doesn't buy that. "I don't expect any journalist to be a 'backpack' journalist where you're going to be doing everything. But I think that if you go out on a story and shoot some video, I think you should be able to come back and flip a print story and a broadcast story and to understand the difference between a print story that goes in a newspaper and the print version that goes on the Web. It's a different audience; it's not the same. Convergence is the ability to understand the platforms and their strengths and weaknesses, and to be able to bring them together to tell the best possible story, and I don't think one person does all of that; I think a *team* does that."

ONE REPORTER'S EXPERIENCE

Novelist and journalist Ace Atkins was the crime reporter for the *Tampa Tribune* at the turn of the millennium when its parent owner, Media General, directed the corporate move to convergence. Atkins had been on the job two years before the decision was made to merge the newsrooms of the *Tribune* and Channel Eight. "We had a lot of older people in the [newspaper] newsroom, seasoned journalists who were not too excited about being on TV, and the question would constantly come up, initially, 'Am I going to make more money if I'm going to be doing both?'"

There would be no additional money for the reporters. Atkins says the *Tribune* justified it by reasoning that reporters would be putting in the same amount of time each day, whether they were spending three hours in front of their computers or three hours in front of a TV camera. It was still the same amount of time.

SPILLING YOUR BEANS

But Atkins says one of the most difficult things for him to accept was having to scoop himself. "You didn't want to spill your beans on the afternoon news and the competing newspaper finds out from you and has your scoop in their paper the next morning." Atkins says that for print reporters, scooping the competition means seeing the story in their newspaper only. "It was a major issue," says Atkins.

Atkins says it became a constant battle between protective editors in the newspaper newsroom on the third floor and ambitious producers in the TV newsroom downstairs. Because staff from both floors attended the four o'clock editorial meeting, everybody knew who was working on what. "And [the producers] would say, 'I'm sorry, we have to have this for the eleven o'clock news,' and our editors would say 'We're not going to give this to you because we want to trash the *St. Petersburg Times* tomorrow.'" The findings of the *Convergence Continuum* support Atkins' observations: "One editor recalls situations in which his supervisors "had to beat on my head, because I'm accustomed to seeing other mediums as competitor."[6]

SEPARATE DISCIPLINES

While the theory is that convergence would merge the two disciplines of print and broadcast reporting, which would be reflected in an enhanced online presentation, Atkins says the reality of his experience was that it never really happened during his time with the *Tribune*. He says he felt it was a "one-way street from the print side to the broadcast side." He says it benefited Channel Eight as a marketing tool, giving it extra bodies and more sources, because print reporters were often brought on live to talk as experts on the beats they covered. Atkins says the print reporters weren't comfortable acting as experts and that, combined with the fact that "print people have a tendency to be the deer in the headlights in front of the camera," made the role even more uncomfortable.

Braseth acknowledges that he is finding what Atkins says to be true to a degree at the University of Mississippi's converged Student Media Center, and adds that no one knows how that will shake out. "What I do know is that when I see excellent converged journalism, it helps tell better stories." He cites Nytimes.com. "It is not simply the *New York Times* being uploaded onto the Web." Braseth says the site's coverage of the World Trade Center attack was presented in a way that traditional media could not match. "To be able to listen to fifteen minutes of chatter between 9/11 dispatchers and the people out in the field, to actually see what happened when the planes went into the building, to hear telephone calls from people whose last minutes were ticking away, to see where the firefighters went up, where they did incredibly bright things and where they broke down, and what they did better than anything else was tell the human story. . . . I was able to grasp the story in a way that up to that point I just couldn't have done. And so you have print, and you have broadcast, and then you have audio, and then you have interactive graphics, and ultimately what those tools do is they help tell a better story and a more accurate story—when convergence is *working.*"

IF YOU BUILD IT THEY WILL COME

"When you build a $42 million facility, you've pretty much decided to converge," said *Tampa Tribune* editor Donna Reed at the 2002 national convention of the Association for Education in Journalism and Mass Communications. Reed's comments were designed to answer critics and to prod journalism schools into preparing their students for a multimedia future.

Atkins says Media General's appeal to higher education does make sense. He says that if you start with the idea of graduating convergence reporters rather than trying to create them out of two separate entities on the job, there's a better probability that what is promised could be what is delivered.

That's the way Braseth sees it, but he says resistance to change is not limited to working professionals. "One of the most surprising things about all of this is the resistance of young people to this change. We're only two months into this, and there's a lot of resistance, especially those with two or three years of experience working with the paper. We have some *DM* [*Daily Mississippian*] people who think they are true journalists, much more so than broadcast students; they view print as a pure form of journalism and some are really arrogant about it." Assistant director Mitchell agrees. "I think the hardest part of this experience has been dealing with the few students that really wanted to dig their heals in against the changes." However, Mitchell says that began to change the day four students died in the ATO fire. "The ATO experience, as tragic as it was, was a true test of our new multimedia newsroom. It helped the students to see how it was all supposed to work." Radio station manager and assistant professor of journalism Melanie Stone cites the case of the *DM*'s student editor for campus news, whose conversion was truly a trial by fire. "He didn't want to share his news with TV, but the day of the ATO fire, such a horrible thing to happen, he was out there, and when Ralph called into the radio station and gave the phone to him to do the update, he did an excellent job, and when he came out of that whole experience, he said 'I understand the value of this. I get it.'"

"That was no small feat," says *DM* editor Emery Carrin. "A little over a week before the fire, he stormed out of a convergence meeting." Carrin says she, too, was initially resistant to the SMC's move to convergence. She says she was concerned about the gap in the news-gathering abilities that existed between the radio and TV stations and the *DM*. "I couldn't see where convergence would bring anything but an even greater overextension of our news editors." The center had only been operating as a converged operation for a week before the ATO fire, and Carrin says she didn't have any solid evidence that it was working. "I knew the television and radio stations had strengths. Their managers told me all the time. I tried to find out for myself, but on August 27, I saw those strengths at work. At noon, Martin Bartlett went live for the first time in Newswatch 12 history. He interviewed me about the scene that morning and continued doing live updates. Before the ATO fire, I had more of a 'go it alone' attitude. That flew out the door on August 27. I was at the mercy of the radio and TV stations, and that was absolutely fine."

Stone adds that she heard similar stories while attending a Poynter Institute for Covergence workshop. She cites the experience of an editor for a Sarasota newspaper: "She said it also took a dramatic experience, a severe storm, and that was when it all came together."

Senior Martin Bartlett is the SMC's news desk manager for Thedmonline.com and an anchor for the TV station's Newswatch 12. On any given day, he could probably count on only a handful of viewers in the small university town, no matter how big the story. But the day of the fire, the difference between traditional and new media was made graphically clear to him. "By the end of that day we had over a million hits, by the end of the weekend, we had almost two million if not more."

Junior Noah Bunn is the SMC's online editor: "Initially the students weren't sure what their role was here; *we* weren't sure what their role was." But Bunn says students routinely come in now for story ideas. "Great example, a guy came in two days ago; he needed to get published for his 272 [print-reporting] class and we gave him a story, and said, while you're at it, take this camera and cover the debate that you're writing about, and he did it and he shot great video. They did a voiceover on *Newswatch* [the center's TV newscast], and so he was immediately into it—had never touched a video camera in that capacity."

"If you say I'm going to hire four people to be convergence reporters, and they basically go both ways, kind of like old football players who play offense and defense, and they're going to make $80,000 a year (as opposed to 35 or 40K), I think it would get a lot of people's attention and that would change the whole base of things." For that reason, Atkins says journalism students would be wise to take advantage of whatever multimedia courses their college, university, or high school offers. He says he can see where students who are prepared to give employers what they want could also be in a position to demand equitable compensation for those skills.

The UM students working at the SMC agree. "You've got to know how to do all of this stuff if you're going to survive in what's becoming the new journalism," says Noah Bunn, adding that it's all about "getting schooled in more than one outlet. If you're a print person, you're always going to be a print person at heart, but you're going to get the better paying job when you know how to design a page, and how to edit some video for it." Carrin endorses that view: "Newspapers will always hire people who can write well. Television stations will always hire someone who can operate a camera or speak without stuttering in front of it. Radio stations want someone who won't bore a listener to death. But missing out on convergence will send you into the job hunt lacking. Plus, it's not that scary and it can actually be fun."

However, these students say it takes more than just attending class. They strongly recommend that you become involved in the hands-on extracurricular operation of your student media center or its equivalent. As Martin Bartlett puts it: "If you as a student can't figure out that you need to be here, you just flat out missed the boat. Go home, we'll see you later."

"Here's the goofy thing," says Braseth. "These people are getting hired, the youngest people with the least experience as journalists, and they are assuming some of the most important editor positions because the folks out there [those running news outlets] have no idea."

THE FUTURE OF ONLINE JOURNALISM

There are those observers who say journalism graduates couldn't be entering the job market at a more confusing time when it comes to online journalism. Many see online journalists as mere recyclers of work created by traditional print or broadcast reporters, and they warn those students who want to originate content to beware.

But Atkins says his experience at the *Tribune* convinces him that online's current viability will only make it more viable in the future. He cites the fact that a TV station's online presence serves a real function in that viewers who want in-depth information after seeing a TV report can go to the station's Web page and get it.

"But right now you see inconsistent effort with Web pages, you see laziness, you see things not being updated, not timely." Atkins says that can be overcome by, again, hiring people who have been prepared for the new medium. He says that when you begin with an online newsroom all its own, then, "you got to have people that are just online reporters, editors, designers, keeping it fresh all day long."

As for convergence, the debate continues with those who feel the corporation is apt to take advantage of the worker, stretching him or her across three platforms and thus compromising journalism across the board, especially in the small-market operations. But others, like Braseth, say journalism will out. "If you look at the history of journalism, it has never been a nine-to-five job; they worked fourteen hours a day. I don't really see that this is going to force people to assume three different jobs and more and more work. I don't think that's the way it should be going and I don't think we expect people to become super-humans." On a more practical level, Braseth adds, "I'm not interested in what corporations are doing. I can't control what corporations are doing; I'm interested in putting our University of Mississippi students in the best possible position for success."

SUMMARY

Just what the future holds for journalism is uncertain, but technological advances have made change a certainty. The student who is prepared to deliver across platforms will doubtless be among the most employable and in the best position to demand equitable compensation—if he can *tell a story*, because no matter what shape the means of telling a story assume in the future, most everyone involved can generally agree on two things— people want to be told a story, and no matter what the medium, the successful story will always begin and end with people.

NOTES

All notes originally appeared in Larry Dailey, Lori Demo, and Mary Spillman, "The Convergence Continuum: A Model for Studying Collaboration between Media Newsrooms," paper presented to the Association for Education in Journalism and Mass Communication annual convention, Kansas City, Mo., August 2003.

1 Craig Johnston, *TV Newsroom Shares Web Site Workload* [Web Page] (October 2000, accessed March 25, 2002); available from http://www.rtnda.org/technology/share.shtml.

2 David Bulla, "Media Convergence: Industry Practices and Implications for Education," paper presented to the Association for Education in Journalism and Mass Communication annual convention, Miami, Fla., August 2002; Scott C. Hammond, Daniel Petersen, and Steven Thomsen, "Print, Broadcast, and Online Convergence in the Newsroom," *Journalism & Mass Communication Educator* 55 (Summer 2000): 16.

3 John V. Pavlik, *Journalism and New Media* (New York: Columbia University Press, 2001), 54–57.

4 Jeff South, June Nicholson, and Holly Fisher, "Cross-Training," *Quill*, July 2002, 12.

5 Scott C. Hammond, Daniel Petersen, and Steven Thomsen, "Print, Broadcast, and Online Convergence in the Newsroom," *Journalism & Mass Communication Educator* 55 (Summer 2000): 19, 21.

6 Michael Roberts, *Let's Get Together: The Denver Post and Channel 9 Work to Turn Their Media Partnership into a Beautiful Marriage* [Web Magazine] (October 31, 2002, accessed February 26, 2003); available from http://www.westword.com/issues/2002-10-31/message.html/1/index.html.

Index

About the Author

Charles Raiteri received his M.A. from the University of Memphis. He is a veteran TV reporter and journalism professor. He worked in television news for twenty years, much of the time with the RKO General Network in Memphis as a reporter and documentary producer. For twelve years, he taught a variety of broadcast news courses at the University of Mississippi, before taking early retirement to pursue his interest in screenwriting. Raiteri has been recognized by the Smithsonian Institution for his documentary work, and has received other awards including the Gabriel, the Odyssey, Associated Press, the American Film Festival, and the Nichol Screenwriting Fellowship.